ADELPHI

PAPER·279

CONTENTS

	Introduction	3
I.	Regional Order: Old Patterns and New Challenges	7
II.	ASEAN Security Problems: Issues and Responses	17
III.	ASEAN–Indochinese Relations: Managing Regional Reconciliation	41
IV.	Towards a New Regional Order: Approaches and Problems	53
	Conclusion	74
	Notes	79

This monograph is dedicated to the memory of the late Kernial Singh Sandhu.

A New Regional Order in South-East Asia: ASEAN in the Post-Cold War Era

INTRODUCTION

From its modest beginnings in 1967, the Association of South-east Asian Nations (ASEAN) has come to be regarded as one of the most successful experiments in regionalism in the developing world. Much of ASEAN's credibility stems from its role in dealing with problems of regional order during the Cold War period, especially its response to the conflict in Cambodia. But, with the end of the Cold War and the political settlement of the Cambodian conflict, ASEAN is fumbling towards a new future. The formation of the ASEAN Regional Forum in July 1993 is merely the latest and highest-profile manifestation of this uncertain future.

One reason for this uncertainty relates to issues of security and stability in the post-Cold War regional environment which have become of vital concern to the Association. This was clearly indicated in the Singapore Declaration, the statement of the fourth ASEAN summit held there in January 1992, which stipulated that 'ASEAN could use established fora to promote external security dialogues on enhancing security as well as intra-ASEAN dialogues on ASEAN security cooperation'.[1]

Of course, ASEAN's managerial ambitions concerning regional security as indicated in the Singapore Declaration are nothing new. According to the text of the founding Bangkok Declaration of 1967, its goals were to 'accelerate the economic growth, social progress and cultural development in the region', as well as to 'promote regional peace and stability'. Although a military alliance within ASEAN was rejected and the security relationships underpinning ASEAN regionalism were somewhat downplayed by its founding fathers (Indonesia, Malaysia, Thailand, Singapore and the Philippines, with Brunei becoming the sixth member in 1984), security management has been a major aspect of its evolution. A number of previous measures, such as the 1971 call for a Zone of Peace, Freedom and Neutrality (ZOPFAN) in South-east Asia, the 1976 Treaty of Amity and Cooperation, the Declaration of ASEAN Concord of the same year and ASEAN's high-profile role in the Cambodian conflict in the 1980s, had both major implications for regional security, and the goal of enabling the grouping to survive difficult security challenges.[2]

The consultations envisaged in the 1992 Singapore Declaration are not intended to transform ASEAN into a security alliance in the conventional

sense. But they signal the Association's recognition of, and response to, major changes in the regional and international strategic environment. The end of the Cold War security order in Asia has been accompanied by new factors of conflict and instability in the region. By holding regular dialogue on security issues for the first time in its 25-year history, ASEAN aims not only to address these problems, but also to lay the foundations of a new regional order to ensure long-term security and stability.

Assessing ASEAN's security role in the post-Cold War era raises a number of important questions. What are the changes in the old regional order that most concern the ASEAN states? Will ASEAN be able to deal with these changes and the specific security threats – internal, inter-state and external – associated with them through greater levels of security cooperation? How does ASEAN's emerging approach to security affect its long-established security framework? Finally, what are the major limitations of ASEAN's new approach in creating the basis for a new regional order?[3]

These questions constitute the central analytic focus of this study and are systematically addressed in its four main chapters. Chapter I surveys the characteristics of the old regional order and the evolution of ASEAN's security role within it. It also assesses how the demise of this old order has affected the security perceptions and outlook of the ASEAN states, thereby setting the agenda for ASEAN's security role in the new regional context.

Chapter II identifies the major security problems facing these states. Four sets of issues are examined: the prospects for domestic instability within them, including trends in insurgency, separatism and political strife; intra-ASEAN territorial disputes; the territorial dispute over the Spratly Islands; and piracy. These issues not only have a major bearing on the regional security environment, but also provide opportunities for intra-ASEAN cooperation, a crucial test of the grouping's contribution to regional stability and order.

Chapter III examines the evolution of ASEAN–Indochinese relations from competition and enmity towards *rapprochement* and cooperation. Particular attention is given to factors which contributed to this process: domestic factors, such as economic reform in Vietnam and the economic opportunities offered by it; intraregional factors, such as the settlement of the Cambodian conflict; and external factors, such as the end of Sino-Soviet rivalry. This is followed by an assessment of the economic, political and security links between the two parts of South-east Asia whose gradual integration is central to ASEAN's vision of a new regional order.

In responding to post-Cold War security challenges, the ASEAN states have not followed any master plan or organising framework. The key guiding principle has been ASEAN's familiar quest for security autonomy, and a desire to ensure it has a major voice and role in shaping any regional-order framework in the light of the changing security environment. This requires a reconsideration of, and adjustment to, some of the long-held assumptions and principles underlying ASEAN regionalism, especially those related to the ZOPFAN concept, security ties with external powers, security dialogue both within the grouping and with outside powers, and specific measures to enhance confidence and cooperation in military–security matters. ASEAN's responses to these issues are indicative of both continuity and change in its blueprint for a new regional order and will be the focus of the discussion in Chapter IV.

This study is not a comprehensive account of ASEAN's functions as a regional organisation, and a detailed analysis of its economic role is beyond its scope. But economic issues are discussed in the context of their impact on regional political and security relationships, as in the case of the ASEAN–Indochinese ties. The study focuses instead on those factors and policy responses that will shape ASEAN's contribution to regional security and order, as envisaged in the 1992 Singapore Declaration.

I. REGIONAL ORDER: OLD PATTERNS AND NEW CHALLENGES

In the late 1980s and early 1990s, the security environment of South-east Asia was transformed by a series of developments associated largely, if not exclusively, with the end of the Cold War.[1] These changes are in turn shaping ASEAN's new security role in the post-Cold War era. The determinants of regional order in the old bipolar Cold War security system were significantly different from the factors of conflict and stability in the emerging multipolar regional milieu. This process of transition has confronted ASEAN not only with new security challenges, but also with a major opportunity for reshaping regional order.

Dimensions of the old regional order
The old regional order[2] in South-east Asia was determined by the two Cold Wars in Asia as a whole: the East–West and the East–East (Sino-Soviet) rivalries. As a region in which the geopolitical, ideological and national-security interests of three great powers – the US, the Soviet Union and China – intersected, South-east Asia was subject to an intensely competitive pattern of great-power involvement from the 1950s onwards. As elsewhere in the Third World, great-power intervention helped to internationalise local conflicts and fuel regional rivalry, with Indochina being most affected. While domestic conflict in Vietnam over regime legitimacy and organising ideology was rooted in the colonial era, it was the competitive engagement of the US on the one hand and China and the Soviet Union on the other which turned the conflict into one of the Cold War's major flashpoints. While the US withdrawal from Vietnam in 1975 marked the end of the East–West Cold War in South-east Asia, another Indochinese state, Cambodia, became a key testing ground for the East–East Cold War between China and the Soviet Union. The evolving Vietnamese–*Khmer Rouge* rivalry engaged the Sino-Soviet rivalry and turned Cambodia into South-east Asia's chief trouble-spot for much of the so-called 'new Cold War' period.

Against this backdrop, approaches to regional order in South-east Asia pitted superpower-proposed regional security structures against indigenous regional efforts spearheaded by ASEAN. Each of the two superpowers offered a framework aimed at ensuring their predominant influence in the region, but also offering patron–client protection to regional actors. The American sponsorship of the Mutual Defence Treaty with the Philippines and the South-East Asian Treaty Organization (SEATO), and the Soviet proposal for an Asian Collective Security System conformed to this notion of regional order within a superpower sphere of influence. But this was not overly appealing to regional actors, especially the members of ASEAN (although the US framework was arguably more successful than the still-born Soviet concept). Fear of being engulfed by great-power rivalry and the uncertain credibility of great-power security guarantees in the late 1960s contributed to the birth of an indigenous notion of regional order, best reflected in ASEAN's 1971 proposal for ZOPFAN. This 'peace through neutrality' approach required commitments from regional actors to abstain from policies that would legitimise external intervention in the region, especially superpower intervention.

Yet, in the Cold War milieu, ASEAN's own concept of regional order became subject to the vagaries of great-power competition and accommodation. On the one hand, the Sino-US *rapprochement* in the 1980s and the US–Soviet détente undermined the relevance of US-sponsored alliances. This, along with the US withdrawal from Indochina in the 1970s and the Nixon administration's urging of its regional allies to achieve greater self-reliance in defence, was consistent with ASEAN's regionalist aspirations as embodied in ZOPFAN. But the latter was subjected to renewed external constraints with the escalation of the Sino-Soviet rivalry. The Vietnamese invasion and occupation of Cambodia in 1978 dashed ASEAN's hopes for a South-east Asia free of great-power rivalry since it had to accept US and Chinese support against perceived Vietnamese (backed by the Soviet Union) expansionism.

In this sense, the two approaches to regional order in South-east Asia during the Cold War were in constant conflict and undermined each other. But what is clear is that until the later part of the 1980s, the prospects for regional order in South-east Asia remained more closely linked to the dynamics of Sino-Soviet and US–Soviet rivalry than to ASEAN's own concept of peace through neutrality. ASEAN had little choice but to be pragmatic and let regional order and conflict-resolution become a function of great-power priorities and policies, even in the case of the Cambodian conflict which became a focus for its political and diplomatic role in the 1980s. Neither this role nor the ZOPFAN ideal could become a viable basis for regional order as long as superpower rivalry persistently constrained ASEAN's options in developing a self-reliant security framework for the region.

Moreover, the Cold War regional order in South-east Asia had the effect not only of internationalising local conflicts, but also of regionalising international conflicts. Thus, Cold War cleavages in the international system directly contributed to the ideological and political polarisation of non-communist ASEAN and communist Indochina. While great-power interactions provided at least a limited framework for conflict-management (as in Cambodia), the ASEAN–Indochinese divide was unquestionably the chief obstacle to ASEAN's concept of regional order based on its professed norms of non-intervention (by external powers in the region) and non-interference (by one regional state in the domestic politics of another).

The polarisation of South-east Asia was reinforced by two factors: threats to regime survival in non-communist South-east Asia, especially in the aftermath of the communist victories in Indochina; and the Vietnamese invasion of Cambodia in 1978. A shared perception of the 'common internal enemy', namely the threat of communist insurgency confronting all its members, contributed to ASEAN's solidarity.[3] However, the Association's exclusivity fuelled suspicions in Vietnam which rejected ASEAN's offer for a shared regional security framework. In this sense, the emergence of ASEAN, instead of fostering regionalism, reflected the existing regional polarisation. The ASEAN–Indochinese competition extended to conflicting visions of regional order. While at the Bali summit, held in February 1976, ASEAN developed a set of regional norms to test the Indochinese communist regimes' attitudes towards peaceful co-existence, Hanoi poured scorn on it at the 5th Conference of the Heads of State or Government of the Non-Aligned Countries in Colombo the following August. While ASEAN saw its role as creating a regional security community encompassing all of South-east Asia, Vietnam perceived it as a defence community.[4] In Hanoi's view, ASEAN masked a Western alliance system imbued with the same ideology of containment that had produced SEATO, and as such, its protestations of regional neutrality and order could not be accepted by Hanoi at face value.

The Vietnamese invasion of Cambodia significantly reinforced the polarisation of South-east Asia. For ASEAN, the Vietnamese action presented a serious challenge to the regional order it had earlier envisaged. Firstly, Vietnam was accused of violating the principle of non-interference that formed the core of ASEAN's regionalist doctrine as outlined in the 1976 Treaty of Amity and Cooperation. Second, Vietnam's aggression represented a threat to the security and stability of ASEAN members, especially in view of the presence of Vietnamese forces on the Thai–Cambodian border and the flow of Indochinese refugees to ASEAN states. Third, as noted above, the Cambodian conflict undermined ASEAN's desire to make South-east Asia a region free from great-power rivalry. The Cambodian conflict was not just a local conflict between different *Khmer* factions competing for power; it also engaged the far more consequential Sino-Vietnamese, Sino-Soviet and US–Soviet rivalries.

Efforts to bridge the political gap between the two South-east Asias were not helped by differing perceptions of the Cambodian conflict and approaches to conflict management. Vietnam presented the Cambodian conflict as a domestic power struggle between rival *Khmer* factions in which the Heng Samrin and Hun Sen faction had triumphed 'irreversibly'. ASEAN, on the other hand, viewed the conflict as a direct result of Vietnamese aggression, which had to be reversed as a basic precondition for any negotiated settlement of the conflict. Adherence to their respective positions saw ASEAN rejecting Vietnam's overtures for a regional dialogue on the conflict and contributed to the prolonged Vietnamese intransigence over the negotiating formulas advanced by ASEAN in international (United Nations) fora. The stalemate which ensued was broken only after both sides failed to achieve their objectives on the ground in Cambodia through their support for rival *Khmer* factions.[5]

Despite the initial setback, Cambodia did become a major testing ground for regional approaches to conflict management in South-east Asia. This itself was a major development in the Cold War regional order since, unlike other regions of the Third World where regional organisations (such as the Organisation of African Unity (OAU), the Organisation of American States (OAS) and the Arab League) emerged with a role in the pacific resolution of conflicts, South-east Asia did not develop an indigenous mechanism for conflict control until much later. Indeed, the creation of ASEAN had been preceded by a number of unsuccessful and short-lived experiments with regionalism, each of them overwhelmed by prevailing intraregional tensions. The earliest attempt at a regional association, the Association of South-east Asia (ASA), formed in 1961, was handicapped not only by the non-membership of the region's most powerful state, Indonesia (its members were Malaysia, the Philippines and Thailand), but foundered over the Philippines' claim to the former British-controlled territory of North Borneo (Sabah) which had opted to join the Malaysian federation. A second major factor was the attitude of Indonesia which not only lacked enthusiasm for regional cooperation, but was also actively undermining the prospect for regional order by launching an armed campaign to extinguish the newly independent Malaysian state. Indonesian President Sukarno's 'crush Malaysia' campaign accounted for the demise of the idea of MAPHILINDO, a loose confederation of three independent states of Malay stock (Malaysia, the Philippines and Indonesia).

The creation of ASEAN marked the consummation of the armed conflict between Indonesia and Malaysia and signalled its founding members' intention to reduce the scope for further inter-state warfare. Although intramural tensions between Malaysia and the Philippines over the Sabah issue and between Singapore and its Malay neighbours (Indonesia and Malaysia) threatened ASEAN's existence for much of the late 1960s, the regional group was able to survive thanks to a sense of common vulnerability in the face of the threat of externally backed communist insurgency. By the time the US withdrew from Vietnam in 1975, ASEAN had succeeded in diffusing intramural conflicts and was gradually developing into a limited 'security community'.[6] Thanks to the impact of the Indochinese conflict and the 'habit' of cooperation developed through regular political, diplomatic, cultural and military exchanges, ASEAN states had come to a point where intra-ASEAN conflicts had 'either become irrelevant or been muted considerably', as Singapore's Foreign Minister claimed in 1982.[7]

In the aftermath of the Vietnamese invasion of Cambodia, ASEAN needed, and had the opportunity, to extend its role to extramural conflicts as well. Its efforts in managing the Cambodian conflict included organising a UN-sponsored International Conference on Kampuchea in 1981, and Indonesia's attempts to break the stalemate in the peace process through 'cocktail' talks with the Cambodian factions which led to the two Jakarta Informal Meetings in 1988 and 1989, both served as essential preludes to the two Paris peace conferences. These efforts did make a significant contribution to the evolving peace process, although the final settlement of the conflict was managed through accommodation between the principal external powers. But ASEAN deserves credit for keeping the peace process alive at a time when the external powers were either indifferent or opposed to any diplomatic move towards conflict resolution. Despite its concerted efforts to isolate Vietnam internationally, ASEAN pragmatically left the door open for negotiations with Hanoi over an acceptable political formula based on the conviction that no framework of regional order in South-east Asia could be complete or feasible without the voluntary integration of the Indochinese.

Thus the Cold War regional order in South-east Asia combined elements of both stability and insecurity. On the one hand, it permitted many serious local and regional conflicts and sustained major intraregional competition, such as the ASEAN–Vietnamese and Sino-Vietnamese rivalries. The Cold War regional order in South-east Asia was also marked by contradictions between ASEAN's desire for regional autonomy and the reality of great-power involvement; and between ASEAN's ideal of a South-east Asian security community and Vietnam's firm rejection of it. In this respect, throughout the Cold War era ASEAN's own efforts at promoting regional peace and stability were undermined by the constraints imposed by prevailing patterns of inter-state relations and great-power rivalry. Although ASEAN was able to manage some of its intramural problems, its ability to influence external issues affecting regional order was limited.

On the positive side, the Cold War regional order was marked by a degree of predictability in great-power interest and involvement in the region. Great-power competition, despite fuelling regional conflicts, did eventually create a framework for their management, as seen in the case of Cambodia. Perhaps the most important achievement of the old order was to prevent the emergence of a single hegemonic power capable of dominating South-east Asia. This function, and the strong forward military presence of the US which the old order sustained, provided a security umbrella for ASEAN states that contributed to their domestic stability and economic growth. Last but not least, the Cold War order helped create a subregional security community within ASEAN which, despite its limitations, was rare in the developing world.

The post-Cold War security environment: a new regional disorder?

Identifying the determinants of a new regional order in South-east Asia is constrained by the fact that global changes resulting from the end of the Cold War have yet to register fully on the regional balance of power. As a result, the regional security environment remains in a state of flux. But what is unmistakable and particularly striking is that few, if any, of the regional actors, including ASEAN members, have viewed the demise of the Cold War order as an unmixed blessing. While visibly relieved by the reduction of global tensions and the settlement of regional conflicts at the international level, regional policy-makers have expressed misgivings about the strategic uncertainties and conflict-creation potential of a post-Cold War order at the regional level.

This is especially true of the end of the US–Soviet and Sino-Soviet rivalries. The end of these two Cold Wars has contributed directly to a substantial reduction in regional tension and the prospect for competitive external intervention which had previously helped to internationalise local conflicts. But this transformation of great-power relationships has also entailed a major retrenchment in the superpower military presence in the region, which in turn has fuelled regional anxieties.

The retrenchment is far more complete in the case of the former Soviet Union which, in January 1990, announced its intention to remove all but a small segment of its naval and air units stationed in Cam Ranh Bay. While the Soviet withdrawal removed anxieties about a much-discussed threat to sea-lane security, to ASEAN states it also had the effect of reducing the US stakes in its bases in the Philippines and contributed to the American decision to scale down its own military presence in the Pacific, thereby undermining its role as a regional balancing wheel. Second, for at least some ASEAN states, the Soviet withdrawal from Vietnam removed a useful counterweight to any design by China for supremacy in South-east Asia.[8] In the context of the reduction of Soviet forces along the Sino-Soviet border, and the significant build-up of Chinese naval power, the Soviet departure from Cam Ranh Bay effectively enhanced Beijing's ability to dominate the regional maritime environment.[9]

ASEAN states are much more worried about US force reductions, despite repeated US statements emphasising its intention to remain a Pacific military power with significant forward-deployed forces. The US policy on force reduction in Asia continues to evolve. Under the East Asia Security Initiative (EASI), the US was to cut its forces in Asia by some 12% by the end of 1992, from 135,000 troops to approximately 120,000.

But in the wake of the Senate of the Philippines' rejection of a new bases treaty with the US, 'additional adjustments' in US force presence in the Asia–Pacific (involving over 8,000 troops) have been necessary.[10] The impact of these reductions on US military readiness and force-projection capability in the area remains uncertain. Although the Commander of the US Pacific Forces asserts that the US can compensate for the loss of its bases in the Philippines by increasing access to other local facilities (such as in Singapore) and can carry out all conceivable contingency missions in the region with the help of its remaining Pacific forces (plus reinforcements from Alaska and continental US),[11] other senior Pentagon officials have expressed the fear that cutbacks necessitated by the loss of these bases 'would eliminate real combat capability' and 'may initiate destabilising actions by regional powers'.[12]

This prospect has served to dampen much of the early enthusiasm for a new regional order which was based on the opportunities for confidence-building and conflict-reduction created by the end of the Cold War. In particular, a possible scramble by regional powers seeking to step into the 'vacuum' left by departing superpower forces has emerged as a major source of concern for ASEAN states. Among the regional powers, China, Japan and to a lesser extent India are generally identified as the three leading contenders for influence, presumably because of their capability to project power into the South-east Asian region.[13] Even before the end of the Cold War in Asia could be confirmed, Prime Minister Goh Chok Tong of Singapore warned:

> If the *rapprochement* between the superpowers comes through ... the US presence in this part of the world would diminish ... If this happens, who will be the regional leader then? ... It will be left to China, India and Japan to contest for the leadership of the region.[14]

ASEAN states note with alarm the ongoing moves by these powers to develop capabilities that could be used for projecting power and asserting influence in the South-east Asian region. But perceptions of who might be the next regional hegemon are by no means uniform within the grouping. While Indonesia and Malaysia have expressed misgivings about China's prospective role,[15] Singapore has shown greater anxiety about Japanese remilitarisation resulting from the prospective decline of the US–Japanese security relationship. In any case, the shift from superpower to regional-power rivalry forms the basis of current security debates within the region; with an implicit consensus that by seeking to balance each other, regional powers may engage in a competition that would make a multipolar regional order much less stable than the bipolar Cold War system. India's recent moves to cultivate the military regime in Burma to offset its growing security links with China is indicative of such regional competition.

Furthermore, regional order in the post-Cold War era could also be challenged by adverse trends in the relationships between the US and two of the leading regional powers: China and Japan. The worst-case scenario is that any serious escalation of the US–Japan trade dispute would threaten the fate of the US–Japan security relationship. As Indonesian Foreign Minister Ali Alatas stated: 'The greatest threat to regional balance would be if, for example, Japan said it was abrogating the US–Japan Treaty and changing its peace constitution so as to become a power unto itself'.[16] Similarly, the state of Sino-US relations is seen within ASEAN as a key factor in South-east Asian security. In this view, the growing friction between the US and China over human rights issues and Washington's threat of economic sanctions against China would make the latter 'angry and resentful' and 'have serious long-term consequences for Asia–Pacific peace and stability'.[17]

The ambiguities marking regional perceptions of the withdrawal of superpower forces are less pronounced in the case of the other major development in the regional strategic context: the political settlement of the Cambodian conflict. The changing great-power relationship in Asia fundamentally transformed the stakes of the major powers in the 12-year-old conflict, facilitating its management. The signing of the historic Paris Peace Agreement in October 1991 effectively detached the Cambodian conflict from its regional and global dimensions although, as subsequent events proved, it did not bring about lasting peace in Cambodia through power-sharing among the *Khmer* factions. However ASEAN took justifiable pride in the localisation of the Cambodian conflict, emphasising that it had 'always, despite the many obstacles, persisted in its search for a peaceful and comprehensive settlement of the Cambodian conflict'.[18]

But more importantly, the Paris Agreement opened the door to the broader process of reconciliation between ASEAN and Indochina. ASEAN, as the former Thai Prime Minister Anand Panyarachun contended, would now have to 'work towards a new regional order that embraces all nations of South-east Asia in peace, progress and prosperity'.[19] Indonesia's Foreign Minister Alatas offered an even loftier vision of regional order:

> One quintessential dividend of peace in Cambodia to strive for would be the dawning of a new era in South-east Asian history – an era in which for the first time South-east Asia would be truly peaceful and truly free to deal with its problems in terms of its own aspirations rather than in terms of major-power rivalry and contention; an era marking the beginning of a new South-east Asia, capable of addressing itself to the outside world with commensurate authenticity and able to arrange its internal relationships on the basis of genuine independence, equality and peaceful cooperation.[20]

A closer and more dispassionate look at the implications of the Cambodian settlement, however, reveals it as a not entirely unmixed blessing for ASEAN. Progress towards 'one South-east Asia' poses painful choices over issues such as the scope and pace of political and economic ties between ASEAN and Indochina and its implications for ASEAN's existing agenda of economic and security cooperation. Furthermore, it carries the risk of intensified intra-ASEAN competition as members scramble for the untapped Indochinese markets. This was forewarned when the former Thai Prime Minister, General Chatichai Choonhavan, ignored official ASEAN policy and invited Prime Minister Hun Sen of the Vietnamese-installed regime in Cambodia to Bangkok as part of his drive to turn the Indochinese battlefields into marketplaces.[21]

In general, however, the end of the ASEAN–Vietnamese conflict is likely to pose fewer dilemmas and problems for the region's policy-makers than what might be called the 'decompression effect' of the multipolar regional order emerging from the ashes of the Cold War. A number of scholars and leaders seem to share the view that the post-Cold War milieu will see an unleashing of conflicts which were effectively frozen or 'suppressed' during the colonial era and the subsequent period of superpower rivalry.[22] The end of bipolarity, therefore, not only means a potentially greater level of conflict in the international system, but diminished prospects for conflict management as well. As Chin Kin Wah argues, while during the Cold War the superpowers did 'share a stake in managing the international order . . . the end of bipolarity can unleash other destabilising forces which can no longer be managed, as in the past'.[23]

Indeed, South-east Asian policy-makers already view a number of recent developments, especially the conflicting claims to islands in the South China Sea as well as intramural territorial disputes within ASEAN, as signalling a new phase of regional disorder. The former governor of Indonesia's National Defence Institute warns of the possibility that Southeast Asia might become the theatre of 'prolonged, low-intensity conflicts without directly involving strong nations' replacing larger conflicts fuelled by superpower rivalry during the Cold War.[24] In addition, there are clear indications that several regional countries, especially ASEAN members, have embarked upon a large-scale arms build-up partly, but not entirely, as a result of intramural suspicions and the uncertain strategic climate caused by the retrenchment of superpower forces. In October 1992, Indonesian Foreign Minister Alatas spoke of his concern at 'disturbing reports of increased arms purchases' by regional countries, adding that 'ever-increasing purchases of arms merely divert sorely needed resources from national development efforts without necessarily resulting in greater security'.[25]

Concerns about the outbreak of new conflicts in South-east Asia assume greater significance in the light of growing doubts over whether the region could develop appropriate mechanisms for conflict management to promote regional order. Such doubts affect the future of ASEAN itself. In 1989, the Foreign Minister of Singapore said bluntly that 'the continued relevance of the organisation [ASEAN], post-Cambodia, cannot be taken for granted. ASEAN would need new rallying points or risk drifting apart to the detriment of regional cooperation and bilateral relationships'.[26] Furthermore, in a vastly altered security environment, traditional security concepts and approaches developed by ASEAN may not suffice; in the words of a prominent Indonesian scholar: 'it is without doubt that the region needs new ideas for a new regional structure and institutional framework in view of the many changes that are taking place'.[27]

To build a new regional order ASEAN must not only find the basis for constructive and long-term relations with Indochina, but also develop new and greater levels of security cooperation to deal with a number of internal and external threats. These efforts must be undertaken in a milieu that has called into question the past reluctance of ASEAN states to engage in security deliberations and the long-adhered-to principle that the promotion of regional order required the exclusion, or minimal involvement, of powers external to the region. It is ASEAN's recognition of these challenges and the need to rethink its security posture accordingly which underscore the importance of the Singapore Declaration.

II. ASEAN SECURITY PROBLEMS: ISSUES AND RESPONSES

The end of the Cold War coincided with an important shift in the ASEAN states' security predicament. In the past, their preoccupation was with internal security issues, such as communist insurgency, ethnic separatism, political dissidence and civil–military conflicts. Arguably, the threat from within was more pressing than the threat from without.[1] Many of the so-called external threats, such as superpower rivalry, the communist victories in Indochina and the Vietnamese invasion of Cambodia, were perceived mainly, if not entirely, in terms of their potential to aggravate existing domestic strife. But in the post-Cold War context, inter-state and external security issues have become important on their own.[2] Moreover, the question of internal security in many ASEAN states is being increasingly defined in terms of its external and international implications, including the human rights concerns raised by the suppression of internal dissent and separatist movements.

This shift has implications for ASEAN's future regional security role. During the Cold War, the notion of 'a common internal enemy' – communist insurgency in particular – helped not only to dampen inter-state rivalry within ASEAN, but also led member-governments to develop cooperative security relationships short of a formal alliance. With regime solidarity no longer influenced by a common danger, ASEAN now faces other problems – ethnic separatism and territorial disputes – which have a divisive impact on relationships both within the grouping and within the region as a whole. Dealing with these issues requires a new security approach which goes beyond what was possible when insurgency and subversion were deemed to be the principal threats. The extent and impact of security cooperation to address these problems would be a key determinant of regional order in post-Cold War South-east Asia.

Issues of domestic stability
On the internal security front, the most encouraging development for ASEAN governments is the decline of communism as a revolutionary political force. With the exception of the Philippines, communist insurgency no longer poses a credible threat to regime survival in ASEAN states.[3] The governments of Indonesia, Malaysia and Thailand have prevailed over local communist parties which once enjoyed a considerable following. The Indonesian Communist Party, the largest such party in the non-communist world in the 1960s (with a peak membership of some two million), was never allowed to recover from its bloody crackdown in the aftermath of the 1965 coup attempt. While insurgencies in Malaysia and Thailand survived longer due to the availability of cross-border sanctuaries and greater levels of external aid, the 1980s saw the virtual end of both

countries' communist movements. A massive amnesty campaign launched by the Thai government led to a rapid decline in the pro-Beijing Communist Party of Thailand (CPT) from a peak of 10,000 guerrillas in the late 1970s to only a few hundred members in 1987.[4] Not long after, the Communist Party of Malaya (CPM), led by Chin Peng, surrendered to Thai and Malaysian authorities and agreed to dissolve its 1,100-strong guerrilla army (the CPM had a peak strength of 8,000 in 1951).[5]

In the Philippines, the armed guerrilla movement, the New People's Army, capitalised on rising popular resentment in the last years of the Marcos regime to swell its ranks from around 8,000 in 1980 to 22,500 in 1985.[6] But under the Aquino regime, it too showed signs of decline. Recent government estimates, although not entirely reliable, suggest a noticeable reduction in the size of the guerrilla army to less than 15,000.[7]

The success of ASEAN governments over communist insurgencies can be attributed to several factors. The decline of external support, especially from China (as part of its bid to cultivate ASEAN's friendship against the Vietnamese occupation of Cambodia), was especially important in their success against the communists in Malaysia and Thailand. The loss of Chinese backing served to neutralise whatever encouragement the insurgencies might have derived from the communist takeover in Indochina. Another related development was greater internal disunity within the largely pro-Beijing parties as breakaway factions turned to Moscow and Hanoi for aid. (This was especially the case with the CPT which saw the emergence of a pro-Soviet faction in the early 1980s.) In the case of Malaysia and Thailand, the ability of governments to ensure rapid economic growth and prosperity was also important in sapping the domestic roots of insurgency. In the economically less successful Philippines, the failure of the Communist Party's insurrectionary strategy for the 1980s, which called for a combination of political campaign and armed struggle (the so-called 'pol–mil' strategy), led to serious internal divisions and purges. Taking advantage of this, the government was able to develop a home-grown broad-based counter-insurgency doctrine (called 'total programming' as opposed to the 'search-and-destroy' strategy inherited from the US military in Vietnam). This combined the military campaign against the guerrillas with efforts by local government authorities, civilian volunteers and the private sector to address the insurgents' livelihood problems.[8] Although the movement remains a force to be reckoned with, its ability to regenerate itself is doubtful in view of what one commentator has described as 'the poor quality of their cadres, a lack of issues suitable for political mobilization, and the inability to define a new strategy for the 1990s'.[9] Indeed, support for the insurgents is likely to fall further following the removal of the US bases and forces from the Philippines, depriving the insurgents of a major reason for their popular appeal.

While armed communist movements constituted the most serious threat to regime survival in post-colonial South-east Asia, armed separatist movements involving indigenous ethnic minorities have challenged the very basis of statehood and national identity in the region. South-east Asia is home to at least 32 ethnolinguistic groups and all the world's major belief systems. Since independence, several rebel groups have organised armed campaigns against the state structure within the ASEAN membership. These include the *Pemerintahan Revolusioner Republik* of Indonesia (in central and West Sumatra), the *Permesta* revolt (southern Sulawesi), the *Organisasi Papua Merdeka* (Irian Jaya), *Aceh Merdeka* (Aceh) and *Fretelin* (East Timor) in Indonesia, the Moro National Liberation Front and Moro Islamic Liberation Front (both in Mindanao) in the Philippines, and the Pattani United Liberation Organisation in southern Thailand.[10] Of these, the movements in East Timor, Aceh, Irian Jaya, Mindanao and southern Thailand remain active, albeit varying in intensity.

In general, while armed separatist campaigns have been endemic in South-east Asia, they have not posed as great a threat to stability as communist insurgency. A crucial factor for this is the lack of significant external support for separatist causes. Although external support has been available to separatist groups in southern Thailand (from Malaysian Islamic groups), in Mindanao (from Libya and other Middle Eastern states) and to a lesser extent in Irian Jaya (mainly from Western missionaries), this has not been sufficient to ensure a sustained armed guerrilla campaign of high intensity. This, along with effective suppression and/or more accommodationist government policies, has led to a decline in separatist movements in ASEAN states in recent years.

Separatism among the Muslim population of southern Thailand has been reduced significantly as a result of security cooperation between Thai and Malaysian forces and greater sensitivity on the part of the Thai government to Muslim demands for the preservation of their unique identity. Islam-based separatist groups in Indonesia (Aceh) and the Philippines (Mindanao) remain far more active, prompting their security agencies to devote greater attention to the problem as the communist threat declined.[11] Neither state, however, sees this as an insurmountable problem. In Indonesia, the November 1991 incident in the East Timorese capital Dili, in which Indonesian security forces fired at some 2,000 Timorese civilians, might have caused grave international embarrassment for Jakarta, but did not signal a flare-up in the separatist campaign. In fact the subsequent capture of the top two *Fretelin* leaders by the Indonesian military may have seriously weakened the rebels.

Nonetheless, a number of general factors may explain why armed separatism might still be a threat to the internal stability of ASEAN states. At a most basic level, separatist movements in the region reflect the continuing 'weakness' of the post-colonial state structure resulting from the imposition of artificial boundaries by the colonial governments on a population of tremendous diversity. In the case of East Timor and Irian Jaya, forcible action by the successor elite to acquire control over territories inhabited largely by people of a different ethnic group was the immediate spark for separatist action. The political and economic systems introduced by, and reflecting the interests of, the dominant community have led to the further alienation of ethnic minorities. These systems have bred the administrative and economic neglect of remote areas, thereby contributing to local political frustration and rebel action.[12] Additionally, the process of modernisation attempted by the ethnic majority to consolidate its dominance over the state has threatened traditional authority structures in minority areas. The resulting insecurity on the part of the minorities has been the basis for a new sense of communal identity leading to mass-level protest action against the dominant community.[13] The periodic brutal handling of separatist protest by the state's security apparatus has served to aggravate and internationalise the problem, as has support from and sanctuary in neighbouring states. Current separatist movements in Thailand, the Philippines and Indonesia reflect all these factors at work, and will continue to be sustained in this manner for the forseeable future.

The problems of national integration and political stability in ASEAN involve not only the position of indigenous minorities, but also that of non-indigenous or overseas communities. Of these, the overseas Chinese constitute the largest and politically most important group. Indigenous resentment against the economic success of the overseas Chinese, especially their dominance of the commercial sector, was an important and early catalyst of nationalist movements in Indonesia, Thailand and Malaysia. Tolerance towards overseas ethnic minorities has differed markedly within ASEAN. The dominant Buddhist and Christian cultures in Thailand and the Philippines respectively have proved more receptive to the social assimilation of the ethnic Chinese. In contrast, the Muslim-dominated polities in Malaysia and Indonesia have been resistant to such acceptance, with religious barriers to intermarriage being an important factor. In Indonesia, government-backed pogroms against ethnic Chinese, who constitute a small fraction of the population and enjoy little political influence, were a frequent occurrence. In Malaysia, where the indigenous Malays constitute the largest segment of the population but not the overall majority, anti-Chinese feeling has manifested in intercommunal rioting, the most serious being in May 1969. The overt persecution of overseas Chinese is no longer practised within any ASEAN state, but the prospect of serious intercommunal violence remains a possibility in Malaysia and Indonesia.

In these societies, rapid economic growth benefiting the majority indigenous community (helped by racially discriminatory government policies designed to favour indigenous business interests, especially in the case of Malaysia's New Economic Policy) have dampened the scope for racial tensions. But such tensions could resurface in a major way in the event of a serious economic crisis. In both Malaysia and Indonesia, the issue of the 'redistribution of wealth' from the overseas Chinese to the indigenous population remains a significant and highly sensitive factor in the political process. In Indonesia, both the military and the Suharto presidency have exploited the distribution issue to gain political advantage *vis-à-vis* each other. For the military, the economic power of Chinese-controlled conglomerates has been a favourite theme for attracting popular support and drawing attention to the substantial business links between the Suharto family and Chinese business interests. President Suharto has countered the move by calling upon Indonesia's leading business groups, mostly Chinese, to sell a quarter of their stocks to credit cooperatives for indigenous farmers and workers. In Malaysia, the issue of redistribution has been kept alive by the debate over the extension of the government's New Economic Policy (following the expiry of the 20-year term of the original Policy in 1990) to transfer a greater share of wealth and economic ownership to the indigenous Malay population. In the government's view, there was strong need for such an extension because of continuing disparities between the Bumiputra Malays and the overseas Chinese, despite protests from the latter's representatives that such a move would undercut the country's economic growth.

The economic boom in mainland China and the related prospect of a greater Chinese economic sphere in East Asia has added another dimension to the overseas Chinese question in South-east Asia. In Malaysia, the deputy speaker of the Malaysian Parliament has acknowledged that provocative media reports about the commercial and investment links of South-east Asian Chinese in China might adversely affect the domestic position of the Malaysian Chinese.[14] The leader of the main opposition party in Malaysia, the *Semangat '46*, recently warned that the growing investment by ethnic Chinese Malaysian businessmen in China might `create doubts [about] their loyalties to Malaysia', adding his concerns about a possible security threat to other countries of the region if a commonwealth of Chinese states comprising China, Taiwan, Hong Kong and Singapore were to become a reality.[15]

Despite the end of the communist insurgency, the ruling regimes of the ASEAN states face a number of other threats which would inevitably shape their national and regional security perceptions and policies. These threats derive from a combination of factors, such as trends in civil–military relations, the issue of leadership succession, the scope for religious extremism and the political implications of rapid economic growth. The ruling regimes in ASEAN states display a remarkable diversity in relation to each of these areas.

The state of civil–military relations has been, and remains, a crucial factor in regime stability in Thailand, Indonesia and the Philippines. The nature and scope of military influence is not, however, uniform in these states. In Indonesia, the political role of the military is legitimised through institutional arrangements on the basis of the historic role of the armed forces in supporting the national liberation struggle and in suppressing rebellions against the nascent Indonesian state thereafter. The doctrine of *dwi fungsi*, or 'dual function', enshrines the military's intervention in politics as a necessary measure to preserve social and political stability. In contrast, the military in Thailand and the Philippines cannot claim legitimacy on the basis of a strong nationalist record. Instead, it has periodically sought to seize power from the civilian government by exploiting the latter's weaknesses and failures in the political and economic arena.

Indonesia's armed forces remain deeply entrenched in a wide range of state institutions, especially those dealing with political, legal and security affairs. But its hold over the regime in power has declined under the Suharto presidency which has undercut the military's economic and political influence over the years by promoting a number of competing centres of influence. The armed forces have responded with populist slogans for greater 'openness' in the political system and by exploiting the controversy over the extensive business interests of the President's family. This campaign does not, however, appear to involve a bid by the military to seize power, which might seriously destabilise the Indonesian political system. But it aggravates the acute sense of political uncertainty that marks the final stage of Suharto's 'New Order' regime.

In contrast to Indonesia, the military establishments in Thailand and the Philippines remain opposed to political openness and reserve the right to usurp power from a civilian government made vulnerable by corruption and inefficiency. But political trends in both countries show increasing constraints on the military's coup-making potential. In Thailand, the bloody suppression by the armed forces of the May 1992 pro-democracy demonstrations, which led to the resignation of army commander Suchinda Krapayoon as prime minister, signalled some fundamental changes in Thai society that might militate against future coups. A major factor is its rapid economic growth fuelled by foreign investment. As one analyst observes, a successful future coup in Thailand, in order to have public support, would require 'a strategy of hitherto untried approaches that combine seizure of power with methods to sustain business confidence'.[16] But fear of political instability caused by coups or attempted coups driving away foreign investors and undermining economic growth has led the middle class and business groups in Thailand to oppose military intervention in politics. While such economic considerations matter less in the Philippines, here too widespread corruption and economic decline during the martial-law dictatorship presided over by President

Marcos have created a popular revulsion with military rule. The ultra-right forces represented by dissident officers within the armed forces are in a minority and are finding fewer and fewer opportunities to stage a coup.[17] The Aquino government survived several coup attempts to push through legislation limiting the role of the armed forces to external defence only. Dissident military groups are unlikely to muster popular backing for their cause except when allied with other traditional conservative groups in Filippino society. Finally, the military establishment in the Philippines, like that in Thailand, is no longer monolithic as a political organisation; interservice squabbles have undermined its cohesion and ability to dominate the political system.

Nonetheless, recent indications of the decline of the military in Thailand and the Philippines should not be viewed as an irreversible phenomenon. Thailand's political evolution has been marked by long periods of military rule with brief interludes of civilian control. It is too soon to judge whether the cycle has been broken by the May 1992 events. In Thailand, military influence remains strong in rural areas where 60% of the Thai population still lives. Furthermore, the weakness in the Thai political party system, a 'nebulous network of cliques headed by individuals who, increasingly, hold sway through a system of financial support and gain best achieved when their party is in government',[18] would continue to provide justification for future military intervention. As the 1991 coup showed, issues such as corruption, inefficiency and 'parliamentary dictatorship' can have popular appeal as justification for future coups. In the Philippines, the revival of democratic institutions following the People's Power Revolution in 1986 has proved to be remarkably fragile. There remain a number of underground groups of disgruntled military officers, such as the Reform the Armed Forces Movement and the Young Officers' Union, who once felt cheated of power under the Aquino government. Although these groups appear receptive to the national reconciliation process launched by the Ramos government (whose victory in a fairly contested election has undermined the rebels' cause), they continue to wield influence through the old system of military patronage and could still exploit the economic failures of the civilian regime. Continued military interest in politics was indicated prior to the presidential elections in 1992, when military leaders publicly hinted their intention to take matters into their own hands should there be widespread violence and cheating.

Like developing countries elsewhere, some ASEAN states have a poor record in managing a peaceful and organised transfer of power. Only the political systems of Singapore and Malaysia – and more recently the Philippines – have demonstrated a capacity for peaceful change in leadership. The transfer of power in Indonesia from Sukarno to Suharto in 1965, and in the Philippines from Marcos to Aquino in 1986, are a reminder of the potential for instability caused by a lack of established mechanisms for regime change. Among the ASEAN states, the succession issue as a factor in political stability is most serious in the case of Indonesia, where Suharto remains the longest-reigning ruler currently in power in an ASEAN state. While Indonesia's dominant Javanese political culture values political stability and obedience to authority, Suharto's long reign and his family's wide-ranging business deals have created popular discontent and undercut regime legitimacy. The decision of Suharto to seek a sixth and final term in office as president has prolonged the succession issue, although the election of former armed forces commander General Try Sutrisno as vice-president, and hence a potential successor to Suharto, might have removed some uncertainty over the issue. But the increased frequency of student demonstrations in recent years, and demands by academic and Islamic groups for Suharto to step down from office, are somewhat reminiscent of the situation during the final stages of the Sukarno era.

Apart from its potential to cause political strife within the state, the question of political succession in Indonesia has serious implications for regional security. The inward-looking and economic reform-minded nature of the Suharto regime has been a significant factor in preventing inter-state conflict and promoting regional cooperation within the ASEAN framework. Political turmoil over the succession issue might create opportunities for radical nationalist forces to lead Indonesia to return to policies of the Sukarno era. Such a prospect is particularly worrisome to Indonesia's neighbours who continue to harbour fears about Jakarta's obvious potential for regional dominance.

The role of religious extremism as a threat to regime and regional stability in ASEAN focuses on the political influence of Islam. The role of Islam, like that of ethnicity, varies widely within the region. This is partly due to the uneven distribution of the Muslim population which constitutes a majority in Indonesia, Malaysia and Brunei, but only 5% of the population in Thailand, 10% in the Philippines and 17% in Singapore. But in recent years, signs of an Islamic resurgence have been evident in all the ASEAN countries.[19]

Islam can be an agent of regime legitimation as well as popular rebellion. In Brunei, where the population is 68.7% Muslim, the ruling monarchy is projecting a new basis for its legitimacy by adopting the concept of 'Malay, Muslim, Monarchy'.[20] This can be seen as a move by the regime to preserve loyalty to the monarchy in the face of rapid economic development and social change. In contrast, religion-based politics is emerging as a threat to the dominance of the current regime in Malaysia, especially as a result of the emergence of the opposition Muslim Unity Movement – *Angkatan Perpaduan Ummah* (APU) – as the ruling party in the Kelantan state. In Malaysia, the political implications of Islamic revivalism touch upon a wide range of possibilities, from creating the basis for a stronger parliamentary opposition to the existing regime to the more radical vision of an alternative Islamic state which has already been projected by several Islamic groups.

For much of its post-colonial history, Indonesia has been able to keep its political process separate from forces representing extremist Islam. Although Islam played a major role in national politics for the first two decades after independence, a lack of strong organisation allowed the Suharto regime to contain its political influence. The Javanese roots of Indonesia's dominant political culture have overshadowed any tendency towards a militant Islamic identity, despite the fact that 90% of Indonesia's 100 million population is Muslim. But recently the Indonesian polity has seen a growing politicisation of Islam. Moreover, unlike Malaysia, where Islamic sentiments have been exploited by the political opposition to strengthen resistance to the current regime, in Indonesia, the ruling Suharto regime has itself encouraged the politicisation of Islam as a counterweight to an increasingly alienated military.[21]

The threat of political disorder caused by militant Islam in South-east Asia could be overstated. In Malaysia, even the APU has pledged to protect the rights of non-Muslims. Although its official slogan is 'Develop with Islam', its platform provides for non-Muslims to practise their religion, preserve their culture and participate in politics. Furthermore, there has been a decline in Islamic proselytising movements, signalling a levelling off in popular support for militant and extreme forms of Islam. In Indonesia, the encouragement given to Islamic political activity might be a temporary phenomenon. Not only have the armed forces maintained the traditional suspicion of Islamic militancy, but with the severe weakening of the extreme left, the containment of the extreme right – represented by militant Islamic groups – could well become the priority of a military-backed future Indonesian regime as a means of justifying internal security measures.

The factors discussed above – civil–military relations, leadership succession and Islamic extremism – are all determinants of the overall level of political openness in ASEAN states where demand for greater political participation could become a forceful factor in regional political stability. Soft authoritarianism has been a marked feature of the political evolution of these states. As Chan Heng Chee notes: 'The ASEAN countries, except for Thailand, emerged from the colonial era experimenting with Western liberal democracy, but each abandoned the original model for variations of authoritarian forms which accommodate degrees of democracy'.[22] Thailand, for its part, has been called a 'bureaucratic polity' in which access to political power has been dominated by the armed forces, the police and the civil administration, rather than by political parties operating under parliamentary rules.[23]

Although the divergent political systems and regime characteristics within ASEAN limit the scope for any meaningful generalisation, political openness and participatory institutions have not been particularly important to the regime legitimation in these states. Instead, ASEAN rulers have presented their economic performance as a principal justification for authoritarian rule on the grounds that economic growth cannot be achieved without the regime's ability to ensure political stability and continuity. But the claim of performance legitimacy contains major contradictions. First, rapid economic growth has seen the emergence of a middle class in all the ASEAN states with political aspirations that may not be accommodated by the relatively narrow authoritarian political structures. A related factor is the limited extent to which ASEAN regimes have been able to reconcile the imperative of economic growth with the distribution of wealth. The ASEAN economic experience is yet to prove the so-called 'trickle down' effect which assumes that economic growth not only eradicates poverty, but also leads to greater equity. Wealth generated by urban industrial development based on the use of advanced technology could produce automatic adjustments to the distribution of wealth in the society as a whole.[24] Not only has this not happened, on the contrary, regional, rural–urban disparities within ASEAN states have widened, especially in Thailand and Indonesia. A third problem with performance legitimacy is the challenge it is likely to face in times of economic hardship. A serious economic downturn might not only aggravate social and economic conflicts within ASEAN states, but also engender serious and possibly violent opposition to the regime in power.

Although the scenario of a restive middle class demanding an end to authoritarian rule has been associated with rapid economic growth in ASEAN states, in reality, the political role of the middle class is marked by major ambiguities. The Thai middle class has already shown its capacity for mass political action, as in the case of the May 1992 pro-democracy demonstrations. But the situation in other ASEAN countries does not necessarily point to a vigorous campaign by the middle class for dramatic political change. The Philippines, where the political system (like that in Thailand) is based on a multiparty system claiming the longest exposure to liberal democratic ideals dating back from the Propaganda Movement of the second half of the nineteenth century, already provides ample scope for open political participation by the middle class within its new constitution. On the other hand, the dominant party systems in Malaysia and Singapore appear to face little threat from the middle class which has made rapid economic gains under the present system and thus has a vested interest in political stability and continuity. This is especially so in Malaysia, where the policies of the dominant party have led to the rapid expansion of the Malay middle class, but not necessarily at the expense of its counterpart from other ethnic communities which have also continued to expand.[25] In Indonesia too, the middle class does not appear to have either the interest or the influence to campaign for democracy for the masses.

The Indonesian middle class is relatively small compared to those in Malaysia and Singapore (in relation to total population). Like that in Malaysia, it is not strong enough to manage a political transition on its own, only when allied with other forces vying for political power, such as military and/or Islamic groups. In Singapore, the professional middle class has been content with a demand for more public information and a role in providing feedback on government policy-making. Although Singaporeans may be 'demanding more political space, participatory government, open government, and a step back from an over-regulated society', they also 'do not reject the PAP [People's Action Party] government nor even the dominant party system'.[26]

As the above analysis indicates, the question of internal political unrest in ASEAN states remains closely linked to the legitimacy of the state as well as the regime. While the Association's members have encountered many of the internal security problems commonly associated with the politics of new states, the degree of political stability enjoyed by them in recent years has been remarkable in comparison to other parts of the developing world. There is no major basis for assuming that things will be different in the post-Cold War era, although the end of the communist insurgency threat will make a difference to cooperation among ASEAN states over internal security issues.

ASEAN cooperation on internal security: the shifting focus
A notable feature of the ASEAN states' efforts to ensure domestic stability has in the past involved security arrangements geared to combatting the threat of insurgency and subversion. These arrangements were a product of an implicit consensus among its members to prevent the kind of radical internal change in their societies that had engulfed neighbouring Indochina.[27] Despite ASEAN's refusal to adopt a military profile, bilateral counter-insurgency cooperation against border-region insurgencies have been commonplace.

Examples include the Thai–Malaysian joint border operation,[28] aimed at stamping out the remnants of the CPM which retreated into Thai territory following the successful British counter-insurgency campaign in Malay. The scope of Thai–Malaysian cooperation covered a wide range of measures, including intelligence-sharing, joint counter-insurgency operations, joint exercises and socio-economic projects in the border area. Similarly, the Indonesian–Malaysian border cooperation was aimed at insurgents on their common land and sea border in the East Malaysia–Kalimantan area.[29] A 1972 agreement between the two countries created a joint border committee with responsibility to 'confer on appropriate measures to be adopted with a view to eliminating the communist threat along the common border of . . . [the] two countries and also other matters pertaining to security in . . . border regions'.[30]

Such joint border operations were complemented by the widespread sharing of intelligence information on communist insurgents on both a bilateral and a multilateral basis. The intelligence agencies of Malaysia and Singapore joined hands 'against any subversive and criminal elements' despite serious strains in their political relations.[31] Indonesia and Singapore began regular intelligence exchanges soon after the end of confrontation.[32] The communist takeovers in Indochina widened and strengthened intra-ASEAN intelligence exchanges. Thailand and the Philippines signed an accord in December 1976 'to continue to cooperate in combatting internal insurgency and subversion through consultations and exchanges of intelligence and views'.[33] Singapore and the Philippines also reached agreement on intelligence exchanges and consultations on problems of insurgency,[34] while an exchange of 'military information' took place between Bangkok and Jakarta.[35] In addition to bilateral exchanges, ASEAN-wide intelligence meetings began around the time of the Bali summit, which endorsed the right of member-states to continue security arrangements outside the ASEAN framework.

With the decline of communist insurgencies, border security arrangements between ASEAN states have lost much of their relevance and are directing their attention towards problems of smuggling, drug trafficking and the management of boundary disputes. It is noteworthy that a comparable degree of intra-ASEAN cooperation has not developed over the suppression of separatist rebellion. On the contrary, these movements have proved to be a highly contentious factor in bilateral relations within the grouping. For example, the rebellion in Aceh has become an extremely sensitive issue in Indonesian–Malaysian relations due to Jakarta's suspicions that the rebels receive material support and sanctuary in Malaysia. Manila's worry that the Moro separatists in Mindanao receive support from the Malaysian state of Sabah has led politicians in the Philippines to take a hardline stand on the formal renunciation of their country's claim to Sabah. Relations between Thailand and Malaysia remain strained over the latter's alleged support for Muslim separatists in Southern Thailand. Against this backdrop, intra-ASEAN security cooperation to fight separatism is unlikely to match the level of cooperation against insurgency. Similarly, issues of domestic political change are not a matter for collective action, although on occasions ASEAN states have adopted positions on issues of regime legitimacy. (Such support was crucial for the fledgling government of President Aquino in the Philippines, and more recently individual ASEAN members expressed their disapproval of the military-dominated Suchinda regime in Thailand. But as the case of Burma illustrates, ASEAN states as a group are clearly opposed to any move that might undermine regime maintenance in a neighbouring state and smack of interference in the domestic affairs of a neighbour.)

While bilateral security measures against the domestic bases of separatism have not proved feasible, ASEAN states are increasingly aware of the need for diplomatic cooperation to handle the international repercussions of their attempt to ensure stability against ethnic separatism or political rebellion. The growing human rights and democratisation concerns in the West have effectively linked the ASEAN states' domestic policies with the grouping's international role. As the refusal of the European Community (EC) to negotiate a new trade agreement with ASEAN after the shooting incident in Dili showed, the internationalisation of domestic issues could undermine other areas of ASEAN action. Thus, while as a regional group it cannot collectively manage internal political problems, the external aspects of political change, including Western pressure on human rights issues and democracy, along with the environment, could become a major new item in ASEAN political cooperation.

In September 1991, a foreign ministers' meeting between ASEAN and the EC in Luxembourg saw serious disagreement over the latter's insistence that human rights and environmental concerns should be part of any new economic cooperation agreement between them.[36] This was rejected by ASEAN. In October 1991, the Vice-President of the EC Commission warned in Kuala Lumpur that failure to respect human rights would have a 'severe impact' on the EC's relations with developing countries, including ASEAN.[37] During the ASEAN summit in Singapore, Britain, acting on behalf of the European Community, sent a message calling for the Association to take action over Burma.[38]

ASEAN states view Western pressure on human rights issues with a great deal of suspicion and concern. Western efforts to link economic relations with human rights is seen as unwelcome interference in internal affairs. As Malaysian Foreign Minister Abdullah Ahmad Badawi put it: 'Attempts to impose the standard of one side on the other ... would ... tread upon the sovereignty of nations'.[39] Moreover, the West is accused of hypocrisy in applying its human rights standards (compare, for example, Saudi Arabia, where the West is backing an absolute monarchy, with Algeria, where the West gave its support to the military coup which overthrew an elected government with a strong Islamic orientation).[40]

Furthermore, ASEAN policy-makers have often argued that the Western concept of human rights, emphasising political freedom and justice, is inappropriate for the developing countries of Asia. A 'confidential' report issued by the ASEAN Institutes for Strategic and International Studies (ASEAN-ISIS), a grouping of non-governmental (though with considerable official patronage) think-tanks, contends that the notion of human rights 'should be seen comprehensively as encompassing a multiplicity of rights ... particularly the right to development and the necessities of life in such areas as food, health, shelter, education and employment'.[41] Given the importance attached to these latter objectives by ASEAN states, argues Prime Minister Mahathir Mohamed of Malaysia, they have been correct in placing 'a high premium on political stability by managing a balance between the rights of the individual and the needs of society as a whole'.[42]

Finally, an excessive concern with political liberalisation is seen as 'inimical' to economic development. As Lee Kuan Yew recently argued: 'The exuberance of democracy leads to undisciplined and disorderly conditions which are inimical to development'.[43] Although this view is not necessarily shared by other ASEAN leaders (such as President Fidel Ramos of the Philippines, who reminded Mr Lee that the authoritarianism of the Marcos era contributed greatly to the country's economic ruin), there is recognition that the Western campaign for human rights could undermine the hitherto favourable economic climate for ASEAN. Mahathir saw Western attempts to link economic relations with human rights issues as a new set of 'conditionalities and protectionism by other means'.[44]

Given the stakes involving economic relations with the West, ASEAN states may see the need to develop less confrontational strategies on the issue. In July 1991, they rejected a US attempt to apply direct pressure on Burma, preferring instead to pursue 'ASEAN's own way' of 'constructive engagement': to draw Burma's attention to the 'world's concern over what is happening there'.[45] But it relented by agreeing to send an envoy to make 'constructive representations' to the Burmese junta. The then foreign secretary of the Philippines, Raul Manglapus, was sent there on an 'unofficial human rights mission' in December 1991.[46] The issue of human rights is likely to become increasingly important as ASEAN tries to define its role in the post-Cold War regional order. The document produced by the ASEAN-ISIS concludes that 'the initial reticence in some quarters [in ASEAN] towards the notion of human rights is now being dispelled . . . ASEAN countries have increasingly espoused the call for human rights, at times directly, at times indirectly'.[47]

Intra-ASEAN territorial disputes
In post-Cold War South-east Asia, a number of territorial disputes have assumed significance for their potential to disrupt intra-ASEAN relations and regional stability.

MALAYSIA AND SINGAPORE
Malaysia and Singapore are engaged in a dispute over the Pedra Branca island off the coast of Johor. Singapore, which operates a British-built lighthouse – the Horsburgh Light – on the island, claims it on the basis of control exercised since the 1840s, while Malaysia claims that the island belongs to the state of Johor. An understanding between the two countries in December 1981 stipulated that the dispute should be resolved through

an exchange of documents. In 1989, Singapore proposed arbitration by the International Court of Justice to settle the dispute, but no such move has materialised as yet.[48] The construction of a helicopter pad on the lighthouse and action by the Singapore Navy in chasing away Malaysian fishermen have increased tensions, and the two countries have on occasions put their forces on alert over such incidents.[49]

MALAYSIA AND INDONESIA
Malaysia and Indonesia's dispute is over the Sipadan and Ligitan islands in the Sulawesi Sea near the Sabah–Kalimantan border. Malaysia and Indonesia cite maps produced under Dutch and British colonial administrations respectively to press their claim to sovereignty. A 1982 accord calls for maintaining the status quo on the islands. In June 1991, alleged attempts by Malaysia to develop tourist facilities on the islands sparked off a protest from Indonesia. Both sides have agreed to let a joint committee resolve the dispute, but a final settlement seems unlikely.[50]

MALAYSIA AND THAILAND
This dispute is over border-crossing rights. Malaysia is seeking the review of a 1922 treaty which allowed Thai military personnel to conduct cross-border operations. A shooting incident in which Thai forces fired shots at the Padang Besar area in December 1991 led Malaysia to accuse Thailand of abusing the provisions of the treaty for frequent intrusion. The matter has been referred to the Malaysian–Thai Joint Commission and the Malaysian–Thai General Border Committee with the aim of developing a 'consultative mechanism' to deal with future incidents.[51]

MALAYSIA AND BRUNEI
This dispute over the Limbang territory in Sarawak remains unresolved.

MALAYSIA AND THE PHILIPPINES
The dispute over Sabah, once regarded as the most dangerous bilateral dispute within ASEAN, is now considerably muted since President Marcos of the Philippines dropped the claim at the 1977 ASEAN summit in Kuala Lumpur. But it has not been formally abandoned. Attempts by the Aquino government to secure the necessary legal basis for dropping the claim has been thwarted by the Senate.[52] A complicating factor is the presence of a large number of Muslim refugees (estimated at 100,000–400,000) from the Philippines in Sabah and Manila's related suspicion that Muslim insurgents in Mindanao are trained and armed in Sabah. This has led politicians in the Philippines to take a hardline stand on their country's claim to Sabah, and to use the claim to secure greater cooperation and assurances from Kuala Lumpur that it will stop its support for the Moro insurgents. Political ties between the two countries remain strained,

preventing the realisation of plans for bilateral maritime exercises and other forms of military cooperation.[53] The former National Security Advisor of the Philippines, Rafael Ileto, issued a warning that failure to resolve the Sabah issue could lead to renewed Malaysian aid to the separatist guerrillas in the Mindanao region of the Philippines.[54]

In addition, disputes over maritime boundaries have increasingly clouded intra-ASEAN relations over the past decade. According to the Malaysian Maritime Enforcement Coordinating Centre, of the 15 maritime boundaries in the South China Sea (excluding the Gulf of Thailand), 12 are disputed, two have been agreed (one partially) and one resolved through a joint exploitation agreement. Of particular interest is the fact that six of these boundary disputes are between ASEAN countries, with Malaysia involved in disputes with every other ASEAN country.[55] The most serious recent escalation of disputes over maritime boundaries has involved Malaysia and the Philippines in relation to conflicting claims in the eastern Sabah–Sulu Archipelago region.[56] In April 1988, the arrest by the Malaysian Navy of 49 Filipino fishermen who allegedly intruded into Malaysian waters caused considerable tension, including military mobilisation by the Philippines.[57]

Despite periodic tensions, ASEAN leaders discount armed confrontation over territorial disputes. As Malaysia's Deputy Foreign Minister claimed, 'we may have problems but they are not that serious to result in confrontation or war . . . We do not at any time ever envisage that we should act tough and use military means to solve our problems with our neighbours'.[58] ASEAN policy-makers point to the existing consensus against the use of force in the region, including the set of regional norms honouring territorial integrity and the peaceful settlement of disputes as enshrined in the Treaty of Amity and Cooperation.[59]

The same Treaty (under Chapter IV, Articles 13–17) also provides for an official dispute-settlement mechanism, called a High Council, consisting of ministerial-level representatives from each member-state. This Council, as a continuing body, is supposed 'to take cognizance of the existence of disputes and situations likely to disturb regional peace and harmony' and 'in the event [that] no solution is reached through direct negotiations' to 'recommend to the parties in dispute appropriate means of settlement such as good offices, mediation, inquiry or conciliation'. But to date, ASEAN members have not convened a meeting of the High Council, despite the existence of numerous intramural disputes. In this respect, the grouping's approach to conflict resolution rests on an assumed ability to manage disputes within its membership without resorting to formal, multilateral measures. Indeed, direct bilateral negotiations have been the preferred mode of conflict management in the major inter-state disputes, such as those between the Philippines and Malaysia, Indonesia and Malaysia and Thailand and Malaysia, with the Sabah dispute providing a rare example of successful informal third-party mediation (by Indonesia in May 1969).

Such an approach to conflict resolution accords with ASEAN's previous reluctance to assume a high profile and provocative role in regional security. It would also explain its general aversion to formal institutions for promoting regional security cooperation, be it the notion of an ASEAN military alliance, or the more recent proposals for a security conference for the Asia–Pacific region. While this may be seen as a weak point in regionalism,[60] ASEAN's protagonists argue otherwise, claiming that its chief contribution to conflict resolution is 'the intangible but real "spirit" of ASEAN', which has been as effective in 'sublimating and diffusing conflicts as in actually resolving them'.[61] In this sense, the record of intramural harmony since 1967 testifies to the effectiveness of the 'ASEAN way', the lack of a need for formal measures and mechanisms.

To be sure, the intensity of territorial disputes discussed above is quite mild when compared to the inter-state problems in South Asia, the Middle East or the Korean peninsula. Nonetheless, ASEAN's success in maintaining peaceful intramural relations was the product of specific national and regional circumstances which have been overtaken by the end of the Cold War. The lack of a more tangible role in conflict resolution undermines ASEAN's claim to be a regional 'security community'. A 'security community' requires not only the absence of armed conflicts within a regional setting, but also the absence of interactive weapons acquisition and contingency-planning in anticipation of a possible conflict. While recent concerns about a regional arms race among ASEAN states may be somewhat overstated (as argued in the final chapter, below), the unresolved intra-ASEAN territorial disputes cannot be discounted as one of the factors behind the massive increase in defence expenditures and weapons acquisition by its member-states. Unless conflict-resolution processes within ASEAN are strengthened, its ability to maintain intraregional peace and provide a useful model for other states in the wider Asia–Pacific region could be severely limited.

The Spratly Islands dispute
The Spratly Islands group, consisting of over 230 islets, reefs, shoals and sand banks, is located in the southern part of the South China Sea and covers a vast area of about 250,000 square kilometres. Although what is commonly known as the Spratly Islands dispute involves China, Taiwan, Vietnam and three ASEAN members – the Philippines, Malaysia and Brunei – the claims of the ASEAN members differ from the rest in significant ways. First, the ASEAN parties to the dispute do not claim the entire Spratlys chain, but only certain islands. The Philippines has the largest claim on the Spratlys, totalling some 60 islets, rocks and atolls collectively called Kalayaan (this does not include the Spratly Island

itself). Malaysia's total claim includes three islands and four groups of rock. Brunei only claims the Louisa Reef, although a 200-mile exclusive economic zone (EEZ) around the Reef would extend to the southern Spratlys.

Moreover, unlike China, Taiwan and Vietnam, the ASEAN states do not base their claims mainly on historical grounds, but on the international law of the sea, including its provisions regarding the natural prolongation of the continental shelf. Among the ASEAN states, the Philippines has the oldest claim to the Spratlys. Its official claim was made in 1955, although the islands were first 'discovered' by a Filipino businessman in 1947. In 1979, President Marcos issued a decree setting national boundaries that included Kalayaan. Malaysia's claim also took shape in 1979 when it published a map of its national territory which included several cays and reefs in the Spratlys as part of its continental shelf (although oil exploration by Malaysia had begun much earlier). Brunei's claim was published on an official map in 1984.

Both the Philippines and Malaysia have established a military presence in the Spratlys. Manila's presence dates back to 1968 and currently occupies eight of the islands, with an airstrip on one of them. Between September and November 1983, Malaysian troops occupied three atolls: Layang-Layang (Swallow Reef); Manatanani (Mariveles Reef); and Permatang Ubi (Ardasier Bank). Malaysia is developing the Layang-Layang island into a holiday resort and plans to build a 1.5km airstrip to defend the island.

ASEAN's security concerns about the Spratlys dispute are linked to a number of factors. The first is its potential to become a source of armed conflict involving ASEAN members, although this fear could be overstated. In 1987, a senior Malaysian defence official predicted that conflicts between Malaysia, Brunei and the Philippines over the Spratlys were 'clearly in the offing'.[62] But Brunei's relationship with both Kuala Lumpur and Manila does not appear to have been significantly affected by the dispute. On the other hand, the Spratlys issue has aggravated the already sensitive relationship between Manila and Kuala Lumpur over Sabah. It is also noteworthy that the non-ASEAN parties to the dispute have adopted a generally more moderate attitude towards the ASEAN claimants than towards each other. In contrast to its response to the policies of Vietnam and Taiwan on the dispute, China has shown a degree of restraint in dealing with the claims made by Manila and Kuala Lumpur.[63] During Corazon Aquino's visit to Beijing in April 1988, China reportedly pledged not to attack Filipino troops stationed in the Spratlys.[64] Chinese Premier Li Peng's visit to Singapore in 1990 produced a statement to the effect that China was prepared to shelve the sovereignty issue and cooperate with South-east Asian countries to develop its resources jointly (it was not clear whether this offer was meant for ASEAN countries only or included Vietnam as well). Taiwan too has dealt 'softly' with Manila on the Spratlys issue, even though their bilateral relations are strained by controversy over the passage by Taiwanese boats through waters claimed by the Philippines.[65] Hanoi's response to the South China Sea policies of both Malaysia and the Philippines has been similarly low key and conciliatory, stressing a common interest in pacific resolution. In 1988, Hanoi issued a joint declaration with a visiting Filippino Congressional delegation calling for negotiations between the two countries aimed at a peaceful settlement of the dispute. A similar reassurance was given by Vietnam to Malaysia in April 1992 when the two sides agreed jointly to develop areas under dispute between them and share any discoveries pending final settlement.[66]

But the likelihood of any agreement on the joint development of the islands involving all the claimants, as proposed by some regional policy-makers and analysts, has limited plausibility.[67] Obstacles to joint development include Beijing's sure objection to any negotiations involving Taiwan, the unlikely prospect that any of the claimants who already have a military presence on the islands would agree to a withdrawal, and problems in deciding the principles for the fair allocation of rights and profit. Both Beijing and Taipei fear that any agreement jointly to develop the South China Sea with ASEAN might prejudice Chinese rights and interests. Taiwan has made no clear commitment for joint development, while Beijing's willingness has not been matched by any concrete action.[68]

The limited prospects for joint development adds to the threat of armed conflict over the islands. Fears have been voiced over the potential of the South China Sea to become a regional flashpoint which could lead to the involvement of major external powers. As the armed forces commander of the Philippines, General Lisandro Abadia, put it: 'there are strong indications that the future area of conflict [in South-east Asia] may shift towards the maritime area, specifically the territorial dispute of the South China Sea'.[69] Indonesia's former defence minister, Benny Murdani, predicted that 'any confrontation in the Spratlys would not be limited to a bilateral encounter'.[70] The economic and strategic importance of the Spratlys is a major factor behind such concern. In the words of Ali Alatas, the 'strategic importance of the South China Sea is . . . beyond question. As a semi-enclosed sea linking the Indian and Pacific Oceans and located between continental Asia and insular South-east Asia, it encompasses important sea lanes of communication and, indeed, the Straits of Malacca and Singapore at its southern entrance rank among the busiest straits in the world'.[71] Economically, the Spratlys are believed to be rich in oil and other minerals, such as manganese nodules, as well as in fishing grounds. Strategically, the Spratly Islands are located near major sea-lanes in eastern Asia which carry about 90% of Japan's oil. During the Second World War, the Spratlys were used by the Japanese Navy as a submarine base and staging area for its attacks on Malay and archipelagic South-east Asia: the Dutch East Indies and the Philippines. Control of the island group could provide a country with staging points for surveillance, sea-lane interdiction and other naval operations that could disrupt traffic from Singapore to southern China and Taiwan.

The perceived strategic importance of the Spratlys and a desire to prevent 'the South China Sea from becoming the next focal point of conflict in the region'[72] were among the factors cited by Jakarta as it sought a role in promoting peaceful settlement of the dispute, centring around a regular series of workshops. Jakarta's motives should also be seen in the light of its dispute with Vietnam over the nearby Natuna islands, which makes it an interested party in the status of the general security environment of the South China Sea, as well as its desire to project its leadership role in post-Cambodian South-east Asia. The first workshop, held in January 1990 in Bali, was made up of delegates from ASEAN member-states only. This was a preliminary meeting designed to consider whether 'the lessons of the Cambodian conflict and, more importantly, the lessons from ASEAN regional cooperation, may prove useful for the solution, or the prevention, of possible conflicts arising in the South China Sea'.[73] It was followed by a workshop held in Bandung in July 1991, which involved the ASEAN six, plus China, Taiwan, Vietnam and Laos. The third workshop, held in Yogyakarta from 29 June–2 July 1992, came in the wake of Chinese action which was considered highly provocative by many participants. This included its adoption in February 1992 of a territorial sea law which claimed the entire Spratlys and provided for the use of force to back its claim. This was followed by the awarding of a three-year contract to an American company to begin oil exploration in the South China Sea in an area just 160km from the Vietnamese coast.

While Indonesia was able to present these workshops as an integral part of ASEAN's general interest in regional conflict management, in reality, none recommended any 'collective' ASEAN position or action on the dispute. The fact remains that the Spratly seminars are a unilateral Indonesian initiative, resulting from 'diplomacy not by ASEAN or even a group within ASEAN but by one member country'.[74] A collective position was left to the first formal consultations on security organised by the grouping and based on the Singapore Declaration. At the Manila meeting of ASEAN Foreign Ministers in July 1992, the South China Sea conflict was the clear focus, resulting in the 'ASEAN Declaration on the South China Sea' which stressed the 'necessity to resolve all sovereignty and jurisdictional issues pertaining to the South China Sea by peaceful means, without resort to force', and urged 'all parties concerned to exercise restraint'.[75]

The chief virtue of ASEAN's efforts regarding the South China Sea dispute so far has been to bring it into the international limelight and imply a potentially severe diplomatic cost (in terms of being cast as a spoiler of regional tranquillity which might also lead to strained relations with ASEAN itself) for any party which may contemplate military action to settle the dispute. But this may be as far as the Association can go, given its ultimate lack of leverage on the major actor in the dispute, China.

While the South China Sea has engaged ASEAN's diplomatic efforts, albeit to a still-limited extent, there is no indication that joint security measures of a military nature are being developed among ASEAN states to cope with the possibility of armed confrontation involving external powers such as China and Vietnam. The only possible exception to this might be a little-noticed understanding between Malaysia and Indonesia reached during the 1980s. The agreement provided for the two sides to develop 'contingency plans that could be put into effect should conflicts in the region escalate to pose a threat to the security of the two countries',[76] and led Indonesia to permit Malaysia to use its Natuna island for military purposes, including joint exercises in the South China Sea. (Other ASEAN countries, such as Thailand and Singapore and Singapore and Malaysia, have also staged joint naval exercises in the South China Sea.) This accord could be a measure to meet future maritime threats from the South China Sea, but the extent of bilateral security cooperation remains in doubt in view of their above-mentioned dispute over the Sipadan and Ligitan islands.

Piracy in ASEAN waters

Territorial disputes are not the only problems of maritime security faced by ASEAN states. In 1992, the London-based International Maritime Bureau identified the waters stretching from the northern tip of Sumatra through the Malacca and Singapore Straits and the Phillip Channel as the single most dangerous stretch of water for piracy attacks internationally.[77] These areas are an integral part of the crowded sea-lanes connecting the Pacific and Indian Oceans. With an estimated 40–50,000 vessels passing through them each year, these sea-lanes are of considerable strategic importance to those regional states (including Japan) whose economies are critically dependent upon seaborne commerce and the supply of oil from the Middle East.

The total number of reported piracy cases in this area rose dramatically from three in 1989, to 60 in 1990 and 203 in 1991.[78] In 1992, South-east Asia accounted for 73 of the 106 piracy incidents reported worldwide.[79] A twenty-mile long area through the Phillip Channel, located in the southern half of the waterway between Singapore and Indonesia, has proved to be the most dangerous area for pirate attacks. This West–East seaway is crowded with conventional cargo vessels, container vessels and tankers (carrying crude oil from the Middle East), all of which have been subjected to piracy attacks. At its narrowest point, the Phillip Channel is about 1.3km, forcing ships using it to reduce their speed to less than ten knots to ensure safe passage. As a result, vessels in this area are particularly vulnerable to pirates using small craft capable of speeds of up to 18 knots.

Most piracy attacks in South-east Asia involve the short-term seizure of ships, and the value of items stolen by pirates remains relatively small. But the problem has attracted considerable regional and international attention as a major threat to commercial shipping in the region. The seriousness of the problem has been highlighted by organisations such as the Asian Shipowners' Forum, the National Union of Maritime Aviation and Shipping Transport (UK) and the Federation of ASEAN Shipowners' Association. A more significant development, from the regional states' point of view, was the call by some non-governmental organisations for a boycott of regional (especially Singaporean) port facilities unless protection against piracy was increased. Indonesia's sensitivity to the problem, in whose territorial waters a great majority of piracy incidents have taken place, also stems from Western media allegations about a possible collusion between its security agencies and the pirates. While Indonesia views this as a threat to its national reputation, the Singapore newspaper *The Straits Times* has expressed concern about the 'damage . . . being done to the international reputation of the region' as a whole because of growing piracy incidents.[80]

But the problem of piracy in South-east Asia does not just concern the national economic well-being of trade-dependent local states or the international reputation of their governments. Piracy attacks in crowded sea-lanes could also lead to serious regional environmental problems. In the Phillip Channel, the average time interval between vessels proceeding in any one direction is about 20 minutes, while the lateral clearance between two vessels going in opposite directions is sometimes no more than a mile. In a special report on piracy, the International Maritime Bureau has warned of a possible ecological disaster if a large oil tanker with its crew seized by pirates was left drifting in a narrow and crowded waterway such as the Phillip Channel. Such a disaster has the potential to exceed the Exxon Valdez oil spill in Alaska. As the report put it:

In one recorded incident, due to the fact that when the attackers left a vessel the crew could not immediately free themselves, the bridge was left unmanned for a period of 70 minutes. Had this incident taken place in the Phillip Channel, a disaster would have been virtually inevitable . . . Disastrous though the consequences of the Exxon Valdez incident were, in one respect Alaska was probably the best place it could have happened in that the area is sparsely populated. Transpose the circumstances to a similar incident in the Phillip Channel and the resultant oil pollution would extend well into the Malacca Strait, eastwards to well beyond the Horsburgh Light [sic] and, given the necessary combination of wind and the tide, the oil could completely surround Singapore Island as well as the multitude of islands which form this part of Indonesia. Quite apart from the pollution consequence, there is every possibility that the seaway would have to be temporarily closed to shipping and the fishing in the area would be ruined for many years if not permanently.[81]

Rising international concern has prompted a regional response to piracy. But, like other areas of intra-ASEAN security cooperation, these measures have been undertaken on a bilateral basis, mainly between Indonesia and Singapore. Bilateral measures between these two states were initiated during a visit by an Indonesian defence delegation to Singapore in May 1992.[82] Shortly thereafter, a direct communication link was established between the Singapore Navy's Fleet Headquarters at Palau Brani and the Indonesian Navy's base in Tanjung Pinang to facilitate the coordination of anti-piracy patrols as well as combined search-and-rescue operations and exercises. This move was followed by an agreement between the two states in July 1992 granting their navies and marine police the right to pursue pirates into each other's territorial waters. The agreement also provided for the exchange of information and coordinated patrols in the Singapore Straits, the Phillip Channel and beyond.[83] The first joint anti-piracy patrol exercise under the new agreement was held in August 1992 off Singapore waters.

Indonesia has also conducted coordinated patrols with the Philippines and Malaysia aimed at curbing piracy and other illegal activities on their common maritime border. A 1985 agreement between Malaysia and Indonesia provides for routine and periodic coordinated patrols organised under the auspices of the General Border Committee between the two states in the Strait of Malacca.[84] Recently, Jakarta has suggested the extension of the Singapore–Indonesian bilateral framework to include Malaysia.[85]

Malaysia has viewed the problem of piracy as part of a broader regional concern over maritime security. In 1992, Prime Minister Mahathir called for consultations with Singapore and Indonesia to curb the 'lawless' situation in the Strait of Malacca and to create a regime for maintaining the security of the waterway, the cost of which would be shared among the users of the Strait. A related development was a proposal by Malaysia's trade and industry minister for the establishment of an internationally sponsored fund for 'maritime security and maritime conservation'.[86] But this proposal has yet to find support from other ASEAN states. Malaysia has also expressed some support for the establishment of a regional maritime surveillance regime to address a number of issues, including piracy.[87]

While seeking external financial resources to ensure sea-lane security, Malaysia, along with Indonesia, has opposed any direct outside involvement in dealing with the piracy problem. This was clearly illustrated in the response to the proposal by the International Maritime Bureau to create a Regional Piracy Centre in ASEAN.[88] Although such a centre was set up in Kuala Lumpur in October 1992 'to monitor piracy activities round the clock and inform countries closest to the attacks the details for speedy action', it has received a cool response from both Malaysia and Indonesia.[89]

Indonesia has argued that since the vast majority of piracy incidents take place within the territorial waters of the coastal states, unilateral measures by the state concerned would be more effective in handling the problem than an externally sponsored regime. Since 1990, Indonesian intelligence and security personnel have increased piracy surveillance in the Phillip Channel, the Riau Province, the Natuna and Anambas islands, the Strait of Malacca, southern Sumatra and western Kalimantan. Jakarta claims these measures are effective in reducing the incidence of piracy. In this context, a regional anti-piracy centre would, in Jakarta's view, be 'wasting and ineffective'.[90] Instead, Indonesian authorities have recommended the creation of an ASEAN Maritime Data Base including information on piracy and armed robbery in the region to be located at the ASEAN secretariat in Jakarta.[91]

Recent reports indicate a decline in the number of piracy attacks in the region, which might be attributable partly to the success of the joint Singapore–Indonesian patrols. But a multilateral approach to combatting piracy might still prove useful in expanding the scope of existing bilateral defence links within ASEAN, as some of its members wish. Such an arrangement would be a relatively less controversial building bloc for more elaborate forms of regional military cooperation. But whether such a step would be taken or not depends on the general outlook of the ASEAN members on the issue of defence cooperation.

III. ASEAN–INDOCHINESE RELATIONS: MANAGING REGIONAL RECONCILIATION

Few issues in post-Cold War South-east Asia have a more significant bearing on prospects for regional order than the reconciliation between ASEAN and Indochina. The transformation of ASEAN–Indochinese rivalry began in the late 1980s. Initially, it was a slow and tortuous process driven by the shifting regional posture of Hanoi's reform-minded leadership, but thwarted by a generally lukewarm response from a cautious and internally divided ASEAN membership. While the *rapprochement* gathered momentum in the 1990s, particularly after the signing of the Paris Peace Agreement on Cambodia in 1991, this was not before it had exposed ASEAN's shaky consensus over relations with Indochina and raised doubts about its post-Cambodia unity in general.

Evolution of a new relationship

Although global and regional developments associated with the end of the Cold War contributed to it, the beginning of the end of ASEAN–Vietnamese rivalry can be traced to a dramatic thaw in its core element – the Thai–Vietnamese rivalry – which in turn was helped by domestic changes in both countries.

The most important of these occurred in Vietnam. In 1986, the ruling Communist Party of Vietnam adopted sweeping reforms to its domestic economy under a policy of 'renovation' or *doi moi*. This signalled, among other things,[1] Hanoi's realisation that its occupation of Cambodia entailed severe economic costs that it could no longer afford. Managing the economic crisis at home to ensure regime survival became a more important concern for Hanoi than maintaining its occupation of Cambodia which had been justified as a response to external threats.[2] The objective of Vietnamese reform – to create a 'market mechanism economy' with the help of foreign investment and export promotion – dictated necessary adjustments to its foreign relations with the objective of ending its international isolation and improving the political climate for economic ties with its ASEAN neighbours.

Initially, the ASEAN states more or less ignored or dismissed the implications of Vietnamese reform for ASEAN–Indochinese relations, choosing instead to focus on Hanoi's continued occupation of Cambodia. Although Singapore and Thailand noted that Vietnam's reform priorities would improve the outlook for a settlement of the Cambodian conflict, Thai Foreign Minister Siddhi Savetsila cautioned in June 1987 that Hanoi's commitment to reform appeared 'dubious' and did not signal an end to its attempt to impose 'military rule' on Cambodia.[3]

But the advent of a new government in Bangkok under the premiership of Chatichai Choonhavan in August 1988 produced a major shift in Thai policy towards Hanoi. Recognising the political and economic opportunities offered by Vietnam's reforms, Chatichai declared that Thai policy would now aim at 'turning the Indochinese battlefields into marketplaces'.[4] Bangkok indicated its willingness to tolerate some Vietnamese influence in Indochina with the hope that the economic liberalisation of Indochina assisted by trade and investment links with Thailand would gradually reduce the scope for Vietnamese domination and enhance Thai regional posture. The new Thai policy also sought to exploit a similar reform process initiated by the Lao People's Revolutionary Party at its Fourth Party Congress in 1986. Called 'New Economic Management', the package of reforms decentralised the managament of public enterprises, encouraged the private sector and envisaged closer economic cooperation with neighbours, 'in particular, trade relations with Thailand'.[5]

But the new Thai policy was at odds with the hardline collective position of ASEAN and was greeted with suspicion by its ASEAN partners. Not only was Bangkok accused of seeking unilateral economic advantage by promoting rapid trade and investment links with Indochina, but Chatichai's political initiatives on the Cambodian conflict undermined ASEAN's consensual diplomacy.[6] In particular, his move to invite Prime Minister Hun Sen to Bangkok in January 1989 caused apprehension in other ASEAN capitals, especially in Singapore and Indonesia. In Singapore, S. Rajaratnam, a former foreign minister and founding father of ASEAN, warned that the Thai initiative could seriously damage ASEAN's credibility as one of the few successful examples of regional political cooperation in the Third World.[7] The military and foreign-policy elite in Indonesia also viewed the implications of the Chatichai initiative with considerable suspicion. The Alumni Association of the National Defence Institute stated that Thailand's 'new policy and strategy [on the Cambodian problem] are regarded by the other five ASEAN countries as violating the ASEAN consensus, wherein not a single ASEAN country is justified to make a commitment which is directed to help Vietnam before a comprehensive settlement has been found to the Cambodian problem'.[8] The critics of the new Thai policy argued that it would legitimise Vietnam's occupation of Cambodia and ease the pressure on Hanoi to make concessions at the negotiating table over Cambodia's political future.[9] Indeed, the failure of the Jakarta Informal Meetings hosted by Indonesia in 1988 to produce an agreement on power-sharing among the Cambodian factions was blamed by Chatichai's critics on Vietnamese intransigence which had supposedly resulted from the Thai government's premature offering of an olive branch to Hanoi.

Against this backdrop, Hanoi's declaration on 5 April 1989 that it would unconditionally withdraw all its troops from Cambodia by September failed to produce a coherent ASEAN response towards improving the climate for ASEAN–Indochinese relations. There was no question that the Vietnamese move removed two of ASEAN's most serious concerns about its occupation of Cambodia: Vietnam's ability to pose a security threat to Thailand; and Vietnam's desire to dominate Indochina as a single strategic unit. Yet ASEAN waited for clear proof of Hanoi's sincerity in making good its promise before pronouncing an end to the regional rivalry.[10] Moreover, differences surfaced over whether the end of Vietnamese aggression in Cambodia was a sufficient basis for welcoming it into the ASEAN fold, both as a partner in functional cooperation and as a formal member.[11] On the one hand, both Malaysia and Indonesia hinted that such a development should not await domestic transformation in Vietnam. As Malaysian Prime Minister Mahathir put it, 'if Vietnam subscribes to the ideas of ASEAN, the system of government it practises should not be something that stands in the way of becoming a member of ASEAN'.[12] General Try Sutrisno of Indonesia argued that by accepting Vietnam as a member, ASEAN 'can rid the region of antagonisms and be a force for cooperation, even with . . . [Vietnam's] communist ideology'.[13] On the other hand, Singapore's prime minister stated that the Indochinese countries should change their economic and political systems before being allowed into the Association.[14] Arguing that 'antagonists do not become bosom friends overnight', Singapore's trade minister stressed the need for the Cambodian issue to be fully resolved before the issue of Indochinese membership 'can be put on [ASEAN's] agenda'.[15]

Intra-ASEAN divisions and doubts over improved relations with Indochina persisted throughout 1990. This was evident at the time of President Suharto's historic visit to Hanoi in November 1990. Suharto, who became the highest-ranking ASEAN leader to visit Hanoi since the Vietnamese invasion of Cambodia, held out the possibility of increased economic cooperation between Indonesia and Vietnam. This prospect was not immediately welcomed by some of Jakarta's neighbours, especially Singapore. The Singapore media warned that 'undue haste in helping Vietnam' might offset the economic and political pressures that had already led Hanoi to seek improved relations with ASEAN. In this view, the Association should 'not allow the potential lucrativeness of the Vietnamese market to detract the grouping from the basic objective of rewriting the history of Vietnamese hegemony in Cambodia'.[16] (Singapore's protests seem ironic given the fact that the republic has already developed significant 'unofficial' trade relations with Vietnam and Cambodia.)

But the adverse reactions of some ASEAN members failed to dampen Hanoi's efforts to improve the climate for ASEAN–Indochinese relations. Continued emphasis on economic reform had increased Hanoi's stakes in better relations with the grouping. From Hanoi's perspective, the normalisation of ASEAN–Indochinese relations offered a number of benefits, including improving the prospects for attracting foreign investment and technology transfers and reducing its dependence on the Soviet Union.[17] ASEAN was seen as Vietnam's 'bridge' to the West; as the Vietnamese newspaper *Nhan Dan* put it, 'the improvement in relations between our country and South-east Asian countries is the most important factor in defeating the hostile blockade policy of the last ten years against Vietnam'.[18] For ASEAN, Vietnam's transition to a capitalist economy provided significant economic opportunities for ASEAN at a time when the latter's traditional Western markets were becoming protectionist. Thus, Chatichai's policy of turning the Indochinese battlefields into marketplaces was vindicated as other ASEAN governments promptly moved to develop significant trade and investment links with Vietnam.

A more significant factor affecting ASEAN–Indochinese relations was the changing relationship among the principal great powers. The normalisation of Sino-Soviet relations, as indicated in former Soviet President Mikhail Gorbachev's visit to Beijing in May 1989, contributed to Hanoi's sense of isolation. Vietnam could no longer count on Soviet backing against pressure from China with which it had a major territorial dispute. Vietnamese insecurity was compounded by the Soviet military retrenchment from Asia and the cessation of Soviet material assistance to Vietnam estimated at some $3 billion a year. Indeed, Vietnam's predicament echoed – albeit to a much greater degree – the concerns of Malaysia and Indonesia about the retrenchment of superpower forces from the region, especially the opportunity it provided for China to assert its regional influence. Hanoi's initial response to this was to seek accommodation with Beijing, but this approach had its limitations given the fact that Beijing would only improve relations on its own terms which were patently unfavourable to Hanoi. In this context, better relations with ASEAN could, from Hanoi's perspective, offset some of the vulnerabilities arising from the changing great-power relationship in the Asia–Pacific region. ASEAN was seen as a valuable political ally against China, even though it could not entirely offset the loss of the Soviet Union as a donor and security guarantor.

Against this backdrop, Vietnamese officials began expressing a strong interest in developing formal relations with ASEAN. In August 1991, the Chairman of Vietnam's State Pricing Commission, Pham Van Tiem, said that it was time to 'institutionalise' ASEAN–Vietnamese relations.[19] To this end, Hanoi seemed keen to accede to the Treaty of Amity and Cooperation in South-east Asia. In September 1991, Foreign Minister Nguyen Manh Cam sent a formal note to his ASEAN counterparts expressing Hanoi's desire to sign the Treaty and seeking a favourable response.

Economic and political factors contributed to a positive turn in ASEAN's general attitude towards Vietnam. Its initial misgivings about Vietnam's commitment to reform were dispelled by decisions made by a

Conference of the Vietnamese Politburo in May 1989, followed by the Seventh National Congress of the Party in June 1991, both of which confirmed the policy of renovation. Politically, the decline of the Soviet–Vietnamese alliance and the departure of most of the Soviet forces from Cam Ranh Bay removed ASEAN's long-standing suspicions about the threat it posed to the security of the regional sea-lanes.

The development of Laotian–ASEAN relations at this stage mirrored some of the factors at work in the improvement of ASEAN–Vietnamese relations. Economic reform had been undertaken by the communist regime in Laos (several months before Vietnam) in order to ensure its own survival and legitimacy in the face of a declining economy and reduced prospects of aid from the Eastern bloc countries.[20] But for economic reform to be viable, the Laotian leadership under Kaysone Phomvihane realised the need to attract greater levels of foreign aid and improve economic relations with non-socialist states, both inside and outside the region.

While ASEAN had not been central to Laos' foreign policy, its economic links (largely unofficial) with Thailand had been substantial and were now deemed to play a crucial role in the success of domestic economic reform. This realisation coincided with developments in Laotian–Vietnamese relations marking a cooling-off of their hitherto 'special relationship'. Vietnam moved to complete the withdrawal of its combat units in Laos from 45,000 at the beginning of 1988 to some 5,000 in 1989 (with an attendant withdrawal of Vietnamese political and military advisers). Given Vietnam's own economic problems, the reformist leadership in Laos no longer saw Hanoi as providing any useful model for its own development. This changing attitude towards Vietnam provided Laos with a greater amount of freedom to pursue a broader foreign policy.

In this context, relations between Laos and Thailand developed rapidly with the lifting in November 1989 of Thailand's ban on the export of strategic goods to Laos. This was followed by a decision to construct the first bridge across the Mekong River in March 1990. In 1991, a Thai–Laotian Cooperation Committee was set up to deal with bilateral issues as well as a General Border Committee to deal with the demarcation of their common border. More importantly, Thailand took action to expel anti-communist Laotian guerrillas who had found sanctuary within its territory.[21]

But Thailand was not the only non-communist state with whom the regime in Laos sought an improved relationship. In keeping with a traditional tenet of its foreign policy – to prevent over-reliance on a single country – Laos also developed closer economic and political ties with other ASEAN states and non-regional aid donors. Apart from helping to secure the inflow of bilateral concessional assistance, this move helped

Laos to allay Vietnamese fears of a Thai sphere of influence in the subregion.

The ability of both Vietnam and Laos to improve relations with Thailand and other ASEAN states was facilitated by developments in the Cambodian conflict, the most significant of which was the signing of the Paris Peace Agreement on 23 October 1991.[22] The Agreement was not without its limitations; while it marked an end to the so-called 'external aspects' of the conflict, namely the competitive intervention of China and Vietnam with Soviet backing, its provisions for bringing peace within Cambodia by resolving the issue of power-sharing among the *Khmer* factions was left uncertain and in the hands of a United Nations authority.[23] But for ASEAN, the accord was a cause for celebration for two reasons. First, the peace settlement conformed to terms set by ASEAN from the very outset, including the reversal of Vietnamese occupation and the replacement of the regime installed by its invasion. Second, the accord was seen as a vindication of ASEAN's diplomatic efforts, notwithstanding the fact that its role in the final stages of the peace process had been overshadowed by the role of external players like China and the Soviet Union. As ASEAN delegates spoke of their 'sense of fulfillment and achievement'[24] for having brought peace to Indochina, the fact that it had been achieved on their terms was the basis for a display of magnanimity in helping war-ravaged Indochina towards its economic reconstruction and diplomatic rehabilitation.

Nine days after the signing of the Paris Agreement, Vo Van Kiet became the first Vietnamese prime minister to visit an ASEAN capital since 1978. Welcoming him to Singapore, Prime Minister Goh Chok Tong announced that a 'new relationship between ASEAN and Vietnam is emerging against a very different world backdrop'. This relationship, Goh added, would lead to 'a more relaxed strategic environment in South-east Asia as Vietnam's economy and policies become more compatible with the ASEAN countries'.[25] Vo's trip was part of an all-ASEAN tour undertaken between October 1991 and March 1992 as a 'fence-mending exercise' and to create a favourable climate for Hanoi to sign the Treaty of Amity and Cooperation.[26]

That this effort was successful was confirmed by the communiqué issued at the end of the Singapore summit. The Singapore Declaration envisaged that 'ASEAN shall forge a closer relationship based on friendship and cooperation with the Indo-Chinese countries, following the settlement on Cambodia'. As a first step, the Singapore Declaration opened the door to all countries of South-east Asia to sign the Treaty of Amity and Cooperation, with Vietnam and Laos being the first signatories, to be followed by Cambodia once its internal political structure has been settled.[27] At the summit, Thai Prime Minister Anand Panyarachun stressed the need for ASEAN members to 'support the economic reconstruction of

Cambodia as well as of Laos and Vietnam, especially through the expansion of trade and economic ties'.[28]

Vietnam's satisfaction with the summit decision was conveyed in the conservative armed forces newspaper *Quan Doi Nhan Dan*, which called the Singapore summit the 'most important conference since ASEAN was founded in 1967' and praised its new initiatives as 'important factors contributing to establishing a new security order in the region'.[29] ASEAN–Vietnamese relations warmed up substantially in the wake of a flurry of high-level visits by ASEAN leaders to Hanoi. On 15 January 1992, Prime Minister Panyarachun arrived in Hanoi for the first visit by a Thai head of government since 1976. The visit produced economic assistance to Hanoi worth about $5.8m.[30] He was followed in April 1992 by Mahathir Mohammed, who became the first ever Malaysian prime minister to visit Hanoi since the latter's independence in 1955. A joint commission was set up to promote bilateral ties between Kuala Lumpur and Hanoi. In April 1992, Singapore's former prime minister, Lee Kuan Yew, also paid a visit to Vietnam for the first time and was invited by Hanoi to become an adviser to its reform programme.

From battlefield to marketplace

The primary impact of these diplomatic exchanges appears to be in the economic arena. Although Indochina remains a battlefield of sorts as rival *Khmer* political factions vie for power in Cambodia, ASEAN–Indochinese relations in general have clearly been driven by the latter's significance as a marketplace.

Between 1987 (when the liberalisation of Vietnam's economy began) and 1990, the total volume of official trade (exports and imports) between ASEAN and Vietnam increased almost sixfold from $58.2m to $337.2m. ASEAN's exports to Vietnam registered an increase from $20.9m in 1987 to $269.9m in 1990, while its imports from Vietnam increased from $37.3m in 1987 to $67.3m in 1990. In the case of Laos, the total trade volume with ASEAN jumped from $48.72m in 1987 to $114.9m in 1990.[31]

Singapore, an ASEAN member, has become Vietnam's largest trading partner, with total trade amounting to $1bn in 1991.[32] Singapore also supplies about 70% of Cambodia's imports, valued at $243m in 1991.[33] Thailand's economic links with Indochina are also considerable. Thailand and Vietnam agreed to set up a joint commission for economic and trade cooperation in December 1989. Thai trade with Vietnam rose sharply from 350.2m baht in 1988 to 2,862.7m baht in 1990. Thailand's trade with Cambodia jumped from 0.2m baht in 1987 to 318.2m baht in 1990, while trade with Laos increased from 1,184.1m baht in 1987 to 2,817.4m baht in 1990. (Much of the unofficial border trade between Thailand and Laos and Thailand and Cambodia goes unreported.)[34] More recently, trade between Vietnam and Malaysia has also registered sharp increases from $150m in 1990 to $250m in 1991, an increase of some 68%.[35]

As with trade, investments by ASEAN states in Indochina have registered sharp increases. With its rich natural and human resource base, Vietnam is an attractive target for investments by these states. In 1990, ASEAN countries as a whole had invested $31m in Vietnam.[36] In Laos, Thailand was reported to be the major ASEAN investor with total investments in 1990 amounting to $17.2m. Although these figures are insubstantial compared to investments by Japan, the EC and North America, the outlook for the ASEAN states' investment in Indochina, especially Vietnam, is bright.[37] In November 1991, Singapore lifted an official ban on its companies investing in Vietnam. In the first quarter of 1992, Singapore's investments totalled some $20m covering more than ten projects.[38] Singapore is also emerging as a major investor in Cambodia, with about 30 projects totalling more than $20m.[39]

Economic ties between the ASEAN states and Indochina remain asymmetrical; while Indochinese countries have not yet become major trading partners for ASEAN, ASEAN states have certainly emerged as major trading partners for Indochinese states. For the grouping, constraints on closer economic ties with Indochina include infrastructural deficiencies in the latter, as well as competition faced by ASEAN countries from other Western investors, including Japan, the EC and, in the future, the US. Furthermore, the economic reconstruction of Indochina will be a mixed blessing for ASEAN. With a population of 68 million and an adult literacy rate reportedly higher than that of any other ASEAN state, Vietnam could compete with ASEAN for increasingly scarce foreign investment capital.[40]

It is ironic that the Singapore summit, which gave its formal blessing to ASEAN–Indochinese political reconciliation, also adopted a framework which would significantly affect the latter's integration into the regional economy – the ASEAN Free Trade Area (AFTA), which is supposed to take effect by the year 2007. To realise the AFTA concept, ASEAN envisages a progressive lowering and harmonisation of tariffs within the grouping to an eventual rate of 0–5%.[41] Indochinese participation in AFTA would broaden greatly its market potential, which already extends to 320 million consumers. It will also increase the potential of Vietnam and Laos in attracting foreign investment.

But despite all their enthusiasm for developing trade and investment links with Indochina, the ASEAN states do not envisage participation by the Indochinese states in AFTA. Even without Indochinese participation, the realisation of AFTA is constrained by differences among ASEAN members over questions such as the speed of sectoral liberalisation and concerns over the unequal distribution of benefits. Manufacturers in various ASEAN countries (especially Thailand) are afraid that the timetable for AFTA is too short; its speedy implementation would see their uncompetitive products swamped by cheaper and better-quality imports from more advanced ASEAN countries. This problem would be significantly more acute if the relatively underdeveloped economies of Indochina are made part of the AFTA framework. Thus, ASEAN policy-makers continue to cite differences in the level of development between the ASEAN and Indochinese states as a key barrier to the latter's integration into a regional economy.[42] As a Thai economic analyst puts it, 'making the Indochinese states members of ASEAN now will be like trying to marry a duck with a hen – they won't be able to produce a duckling nor a chick – you might get a "chickling" but that is not functional, to say the least'.[43] Singapore's Trade Minister, Lee Hsien Loong, listed a number of obstacles to Vietnamese membership of ASEAN including 'differing economic management styles, living standards and integration into the world economy'.[44]

Thus, accelerated economic development in Indochina supported by the continued commitment of the Vietnamese leadership to market-oriented reform remains an essential precondition of ASEAN–Indochinese economic relations. In the meantime, the major contribution of ASEAN–Indochinese economic relations has been to act as a catalyst for political relations and improve the general climate for a security framework for the entire region.

From common prosperity to common security?

One of the most important developments in this regard is the gradual but unmistakable convergence of security perspectives between ASEAN and Vietnam. In the words of a Vietnamese scholar, Hanoi's approach to security up until now was based on 'the old conception which advocated that a country should stand with one great power to oppose another one or neighbouring countries'. This approach conflicted with ASEAN's professed objective of ZOPFAN, which called for regional non-alignment. Hanoi's new approach to regional order is cast differently. As its Assistant Foreign Minister Tran Huy Chung stated, 'what is most beneficial to the South-east Asian countries is to have appropriately balanced relationships with great powers outside the region, with a view to resolving disputes for influence between them over the region'.[45] This desire for an 'appropriately balanced relationship' is indicative of Hanoi's need for a regional balance of power to offset the perceived threat of Chinese domination. This is also consistent with ASEAN's recent move to jettison the ZOPFAN approach in favour of a balanced relationship among external powers to prevent any single regional power from filling the power vacuum created by superpower retrenchment.

On a more specific issue, Hanoi has lost no time in publicising the 'common fear of Chinese policy in the South China Sea' shared by certain

ASEAN members.⁴⁶ Hanoi has openly welcomed the Association's position on the issue which, in urging the parties to renounce the use of force, appears to have been largely directed at China. Vietnamese leaders have gone as far as to suggest that ASEAN's decision to see Vietnam become part of the grouping was due to 'economic and defence reasons', and was linked to ASEAN's fears about China's aggressive posture over the Spratly Islands dispute.⁴⁷ Hanoi clearly hopes to find common ground with Malaysia and Indonesia, both of which harbour deep suspicions of China's naval build-up and its potential to use force in the South China Sea.

But the process of ASEAN–Indochinese reconciliation is less likely to be governed by a common security imperative than by functional cooperation featuring an incremental and 'modest approach to institution-building'.⁴⁸ The accession by Vietnam and Laos to the Treaty of Amity and Cooperation at the Manila ASEAN Foreign Ministers' Meeting in July 1992⁴⁹ is a helpful first step. For ASEAN, the chief benefit of the move has been to commit the Indochinese states to the regional 'code of conduct' on territorial integrity and the peaceful resolution of disputes. In this sense, ASEAN's role is similar to its impact in building intraregional trust and confidence in the wake of the Indonesia–Malaysia confrontation.

But a fully-fledged political and security partnership between ASEAN and Indochina remains hostage to a number of factors. While Vietnam is enthusiastic about the positive impact of a more inclusive ASEAN, it might also be uneasy about trends towards higher levels of defence spending and force modernisation in its states. In March 1992, the *Nhan Dan* reacted sharply to a speech by Singapore's defence minister which identified Vietnam as a potential threat to regional stability. The reaction revealed Vietnam's suspicions about Singapore's offer of military facilities to the US and stressed the need for regional countries to cut their defence expenditures.⁵⁰ Another uncertain element in the evolving ASEAN–Vietnamese relationship is the latter's attitude towards proposals for greater defence cooperation among the ASEAN states. In the past, Vietnam has been wary of such ideas, although given the changing circumstances, such cooperation may be seen by Hanoi as a useful counter to Chinese military power. Within ASEAN, the Thai military remains suspicious of Vietnam's strategic intentions, despite the pragmatic approach of both countries to bilateral relations.⁵¹ Thailand is also wary of the possibility of a major improvement in Sino-Vietnamese relations, which would weaken Bangkok's ability to extend its influence over Indochina.

In addition, there are several outstanding contentious issues between Vietnam and some ASEAN member-states, notably Malaysia and Indonesia, which may complicate ASEAN–Indochinese reconciliation. Malaysia demands a fixed timetable for the repatriation of some 11,500 Vietnamese boat people in Malaysia. Indonesia and Vietnam are involved in a sovereignty dispute over the Natuna islands which once led Indonesia to talk of the 'possibility of facing a sea battle in the South China Sea'.[52] Thailand and Vietnam contest maritime boundaries in the Gulf of Thailand, although in February 1992 Hanoi publicly stated its wish to reach an agreement on the joint development of disputed areas similar to one it had negotiated with Malaysia.[53] Little progress has been made in resolving the border demarcation dispute between Thailand and Laos, an issue which led to armed conflict between the two countries twice in the last decade. Finally, disputed sovereignty over the Spratly Islands also bears on relations between Vietnam and three ASEAN claimants – Malaysia, the Philippines and Brunei – although, as will be discussed in the next chapter, Hanoi has taken a generally more conciliatory attitude towards the ASEAN claimants than Beijing.

The process of regional reconciliation between ASEAN and the Indochinese states might be disrupted by developments in Cambodia's internal conflict. The successful May 1993 elections in Cambodia, supervised by the UN, did not bring about a comprehensive political solution as envisaged by the Paris Peace Agreement, although they did avoid large-scale *Khmer Rouge* violence. While the elections were deemed 'free and fair' by international observers, the United Nations Transitional Authority in Cambodia (UNTAC) failed to ensure a 'neutral political atmosphere' for them. The refusal of the *Khmer Rouge* to disarm, as well as its boycott of the elections, suggests its determination to continue to seek power by exploiting issues such as Cambodia's economic problems and the presence of ethnic Vietnamese there. Failure by the new regime in Cambodia to create a viable constitutional process and ensure economic development might play into the hands of the *Khmer Rouge* and lead to renewed civil war in the country. Moreover, unless managed carefully by the regional and international communities, the Cambodian factional struggle might reopen the country to external intervention. This would not only affect ASEAN's relations with Vietnam (depending on the latter's response to the persecution of ethnic Vietnamese by the *Khmer Rouge*), but also Cambodia's own entry into ASEAN. As such, the vision of 'one South-east Asia' resulting from full ASEAN membership for all three Indochinese states, as well as Burma, is a long way from becoming a reality.

In this context, it is noteworthy that since the Paris Agreement, ASEAN members have been reluctant to take a common position on the Cambodian political process under the supervision of UNTAC (with the exception of opposition to sanctions against the *Khmer Rouge* and the proposal for a presidential election in Cambodia). Nor have they developed any joint programme for extending economic and political support for reconstruction in Indochina.[54] The ASEAN summit in Singapore was noticeably silent on a long-term ASEAN strategy for Indochina.[55] Although recent Thai policy towards Indochina has been more 'subtle and sophisticated' than that of former Prime Minister Chatichai Choonhavan, there is a lingering risk that the development of ASEAN's relations with Indochina may still prove internally divisive.[56] This was indicated in a warning issued by Malaysia's Foreign Minister Ahmad Badawi, who called upon ASEAN members to 'ensure that regional engagement strengthens rather than weakens it, builds upon successes rather than undermines it, and preserves ASEAN cohesion instead of diluting it'.[57]

While ASEAN has made significant progress towards ending the ideological polarisation in South-east Asia, a different sort of division might emerge as a result of the inevitable reordering of foreign-policy priorities by ASEAN states following the localisation of the Cambodian conflict. The concept of *Suwannaphum*, or 'Golden Peninsula', developed by Chatichai Choonhavan, suggests a belief among sections of the Thai elite that Thailand could become the core of a continental segment of South-east Asia comprising the three Indochinese states and Burma. In this domain, Thailand would aspire to be the principal engine of growth as well as the leading nation in shaping foreign-policy and national-security priorities. Such a segment of South-east Asia might compete with a maritime domain comprising Indonesia (as the political leader), Malaysia and Singapore (as the financial and communications hub).[58] If this division is pushed to its extreme by a scramble for Indochinese markets and lack of cooperation and coordination in the Indochina policy of ASEAN members, the goal of reordering South-east Asia would acquire an ironic and perverse meaning.

IV. TOWARDS A NEW REGIONAL ORDER: APPROACHES AND PROBLEMS

Among the principles central to ASEAN's approach to regional order, the emphasis on regional autonomy has been the most crucial and perhaps the most controversial. While the early years of ASEAN were marked by a divisive intramural debate on the usefulness of external security guarantees, there was a general consensus on the need for greater self-reliance in managing the region's security problems. As Adam Malik, Indonesia's former foreign minister and a founding father of ASEAN, wrote in 1975:

> Regional problems, i.e. those having a direct bearing upon the region concerned, should be accepted as being of primary concern to that region itself. Mutual consultations and cooperation among the countries of the region in facing these problems may . . . lead to the point where the views of the region are accorded the primacy they deserve in the search for solution.[1]

But ASEAN's commitment to intramural consultations and dialogue never extended to issues directly affecting regional security. To be sure, the concept of ZOPFAN and the grouping's diplomatic role in the Cambodian conflict during the 1980s could be seen as efforts to provide 'regional solutions' to important regional problems. But the ASEAN members steadfastly refused to engage in formal and regular consultations over security issues. Regional defence cooperation among the members was permitted only at a bilateral level.

Several factors explained ASEAN's reluctance to engage in formal multilateral security consultations and collaboration. First, its founding fathers were sensitive to it being perceived as a successor (however cleverly disguised) to the defunct US-sponsored military alliance, SEATO. The latter had been a favourite target for attack by communist powers such as China and the former Soviet Union, and any security role for ASEAN, it was feared, would lead to provocative comparisons with SEATO, given the ASEAN members' generally pro-Western security orientation. ASEAN, as Malaysia's then Prime Minister Hussein Onn noted in 1976, wanted to maintain the image of 'a non-ideological, non-military and non-antagonistic grouping'.[2]

Second, meaningful security collaboration within the ASEAN framework was neither feasible nor desirable in view of the differing external threat perceptions of the member-states, their lack of self-reliance in defence and unresolved bilateral disputes which threatened the viability of the nascent regional grouping. Thus, while ASEAN clearly hoped to develop political functions to diffuse intraregional tensions and achieve collective diplomatic leverage *vis-à-vis* outside powers, it was careful to avoid any impression of a security alliance.

The development of the ZOPFAN framework was clearly related to this goal. Unlike Cold War alliances like SEATO, which served to legitimise the role of external powers in regional security, ZOPFAN's aim was to minimise the scope for such involvement, especially by the superpowers and China. ZOPFAN was a political concept which enabled ASEAN states to project the image of an autonomy-seeking regional community without the need for formal security functions characteristic of a traditional alliance. But in the post-Cold War security environment, ASEAN's position on security collaboration and regional autonomy appears to be headed for a major shift. The new thinking on security is indicated in several developments, including a revisionist outlook on the relevance of ZOPFAN, closer security links with outside powers, a decision to institute a regional dialogue on security, and evolving patterns of security collaboration among member-states.

Rethinking ZOPFAN
The reconsideration of ZOPFAN is a central element of ASEAN's changing approach to regional order. As noted earlier, ZOPFAN reflected the grouping's desire to insulate the region from the dynamics of great-power rivalry. But ZOPFAN was also the product of a specific set of circumstances which shaped ASEAN's collective security concerns in the late 1960s and early 1970s. Among these were the prospective withdrawal of British forces east of Suez, and the promulgation of the so-called 'Nixon Doctrine' which ruled out future American military involvement in a land war in Asia and urged its Asian allies to accept the primary burden of their own defence with only indirect US assistance. In this context, ASEAN's declining faith in the availability and utility of external security guarantees was perhaps a more important factor behind its desire for security autonomy than any consensus regarding the dangers of superpower rivalry.

The ZOPFAN concept featured an explicit call for regional autonomy by restating ASEAN's earlier (in the Bangkok Declaration) promise to ensure the region's 'stability and security from external interference in any form or manifestation'. The mechanism envisaged by ZOPFAN to realise this goal consisted of two elements. The first required external powers to guarantee the neutral status of the region by 'refrain[ing] from forging alliances with the neutralised states, stationing armed forces on their territory, and using their presence to subvert or interfere in any other way with other countries'.[3] The second element required regional countries to abstain from military alliances with the great powers and prevent the establishment of foreign military bases on their soil. The ZOPFAN concept also emphasised the need for the regional countries to 'respect one another's sovereignty and territorial integrity, and not participate in activities likely to directly or indirectly threaten the security of another'.[4]

As it turned out, implementation of ZOPFAN was seriously undermined by several factors. These included intramural disagreements within ASEAN (with Singapore and Thailand stressing the need for external security links as opposed to the pro-neutralisation views of Malaysia and Indonesia) as well as ASEAN's failure to secure support for it from the key extraregional powers, the US and Japan. But these obstacles to ZOPFAN were obscured by the outbreak of the Cambodian conflict and the accompanying revival of great-power rivalry (Sino-Soviet) in South-east Asia. For a long time, ASEAN held on to the convenient position that the realisation of ZOPFAN could only come after the resolution of the Cambodian conflict.

The fate of ZOPFAN was mirrored in a subsequent but related proposal for establishing a nuclear weapons-free zone in South-east Asia (SEANWFZ). This proposal was first considered at the meeting of ASEAN foreign ministers (the ASEAN Ministers' Meeting or AMM) in July 1984. Given that there were no nuclear powers among the regional countries, the security benefit of SEANWFZ lay mainly in restricting the nuclear options of global powers. As such, it was presented by ASEAN as a step towards the realisation of ZOPFAN, although, unlike that of ZOPFAN, the realisation of SEANWFZ did not depend upon the settlement of the Cambodian conflict. But the proposal was strongly resisted by the US on the grounds that it would cover ASEAN states only and restrict US military deployments in the region. In the US view, the SEANWFZ would undermine its nuclear deterrence posture without imposing similar constraints on the Soviet Union and its regional ally, Vietnam. It was also undermined by the ambivalent attitude of ASEAN members Thailand, the Philippines and Singapore. While the former two states remained tied to the US defence umbrella through bilateral security treaties, Singapore's strong belief in the US role as a regional balancer conflicted with Indonesia and Malaysia's preference for a non-aligned regional security framework. In the end, the SEANWFZ proposal remained ill-defined, with few specifics as to the area to be covered by the proposed zone, the kind of nuclear activities to be prohibited by it, its impact on security arrangements between ASEAN members and external powers, and problems of verification and compliance. Furthermore, intramural differences within ASEAN as well as the adverse US reaction meant that the political costs of SEANWFZ could outweigh its potential benefits for regional security.[5]

As the Cold War drew to an end, ASEAN maintained its official adherence to ZOPFAN. A special task force set up by the Singapore AMM in 1987 called for moves to 'revitalise' the ZOPFAN concept.[6] But as the circumstances which shaped the need for ZOPFAN as a security framework have begun to alter significantly as a result of recent regional and global developments, questions about its continued relevance have also begun to emerge.

Such questions focus on two aspects: whether ZOPFAN is still a practical notion; and whether it is desirable as a framework for regional security and order. Arguments that ZOPFAN is not a practicable concept questions its chief underlying assumption: that South-east Asia as a region can somehow be insulated from the interests and interactions of major external powers.[7] Apart from the fact that ZOPFAN has never been, and is unlikely to be, accepted by outside powers, the argument for a neutral South-east Asia contains a major contradiction. It requires South-east Asian countries to maintain an insular security posture while at the same time exploiting the pay-offs of closer economic interdependence within the wider Asia–Pacific region in which are located four of the world's major powers. The fact of regional economic integration, combined with the end of the global strategic competition between the US and the former Soviet Union, considerably reduces the rationale of neutrality in Europe. South-east Asia can hardly be an exception.

Arguments that ZOPFAN may be undesirable, or even detrimental, to ASEAN's security interests stress the need for the region to retain the 'balancing wheel' role of the US in the interests of its future security, stability and economic progress. This attitude is especially true of Singapore, but generally accords with the strategic perspectives of other ASEAN members as a whole. In addition, Singapore is concerned that by constraining the role of outside powers, ZOPFAN would suit the designs of regional powers, including Indonesia, to play a dominant role in the region. ZOPFAN would thus not only undermine the balance of power among external players, but would also upset the delicate equilibrium in intraregional relations which has sustained ASEAN for so long.

Intra-ASEAN differences over ZOPFAN, evident in the early stages of the Association, have found their way into more recent deliberations over its relevance.[8] In contrast to the attitudes of Singapore and Thailand, Indonesia is clearly reluctant to abandon ZOPFAN as a framework for regional security. Foreign Minister Ali Alatas views it as 'an evolutionary process', representing 'the regional, multilateral framework within which it is hoped to promote national and regional resilience and to seek the disentanglement of the region from the contending strategic designs of the great powers'.[9] But a closer reading of the positions of Malaysia and Indonesia would suggest that neither views the implementation of ZOPFAN in its original form as a feasible response to the challenge of the post-Cold War regional order. Malaysia appeared to move away from ZOPFAN by promoting the 1976 Treaty of Amity and Cooperation as the more appropriate instrument for ASEAN's dealings with the Indochinese states and external powers.[10] Similarly, Indonesia has accepted the need for adjustments to the ZOPFAN concept in the light of a changing regional strategic environment.[11] As Alatas conceded, South-east Asian countries 'can't keep the four powers [the US, Japan, China and the former Soviet Union] out of the region'. The implication is that regional security would best be ensured not through a framework excluding the great powers as envisaged by ZOPFAN, but through 'equilibrium among them and between them and South-east Asia'.[12]

External security links

A closely related development is the growing compatibility between ZOPFAN and the external security ties of the ASEAN members. Despite, or perhaps because of, the removal of US military bases from the Philippines, other ASEAN states, including Singapore, Brunei, Malaysia and Indonesia, have moved to increase defence cooperation with the US.

Singapore, a leading exponent of the post-Cold War 'power vacuum' theory, led the way when it announced in 1989 an offer to provide military facilities to the US, ostensibly in response to the call by the Philippines for greater 'burden-sharing' within ASEAN to ensure the continued forward deployment of US forces. Undeterred by criticisms from sections within Malaysia that such a move would contradict the spirit of ZOPFAN, Singapore signed a memorandum of understanding with the US in November 1990 which provided for the deployment of American aircraft (on a rotational basis) and military personnel in Singapore. During US President George Bush's visit to Singapore on 3–5 January 1992, the two countries reached agreement on the relocation of a major naval logistics facility from Subic Bay to Singapore. This facility, the 'Command Task Force 73' (CTF73), consists of about 200 personnel and would be responsible for port calls and the resupply of US navy ships and would coordinate warship deployments in the Pacific region.[13]

Malaysia has also stepped up its defence cooperation with the US. In April 1992 it was revealed by media sources that Malaysia and the US had been cooperating quietly on military matters within the framework of an agreement on Bilateral Training and Education Cooperation signed in January 1984 (the agreement had been kept secret at Malaysia's request). Indeed, during the 1980s, the frequency of joint exercises between the two countries, involving naval, air and ground forces, had reached an average of one exercise per month.[14] After acknowledging the secret arrangement, Malaysian officials declared that the 'coverage, frequency and type of assets involved' in bilateral military cooperation with the US would be expanded.[15] The status of exercises between Malaysian and US army units would be raised from command-post to field-training exercises involving company-size units. Malaysia has also offered facilities for the maintenance of US Air Force C-130 aircraft at Subang airport on a commercial basis. A deal for US Navy ships to use the Lumut ship repair facility could be worth $40–50m.[16] In addition, Malaysia has agreed to host joint exercises as well as to provide sports and recreational facilities for the US Navy at Lumut.[17]

Brunei has followed Singapore in signing a memorandum of understanding allowing for several US warship visits and joint training with Bruneian forces.[18] The scope of US–Brunei defence cooperation is more limited than that between US and Singapore, due to Brunei's lack of adequate port and air facilities. Even more significant is the changing attitude of Indonesia which has 'fully agreed' with Singapore's offer of military facilities to the US and plans to conduct joint naval and possibly air exercises with US forces.[19] Indonesia has also offered facilities for ship repair at Surabaya to the US Navy's 7th Fleet. Thailand, a US treaty ally, has held joint exercises with US forces since the early 1970s. Recently, Bangkok allowed its airports to be used for the refuelling and maintenance of US military aircraft.[20] Manila is also considering providing some form of access to US forces in the region on a commercial basis and has asserted, to Washington's dismay, its right to seek US help in case of attack on its disputed territories in the South China Sea under their mutual defence treaty.

Meanwhile, moves have been afoot to strengthen the only active multilateral alliance framework within South-east Asia, the Five Power Defence Arrangements (FPDA) involving Malaysia, Singapore, Britain, Australia and New Zealand.[21] Although the FPDA's credibility as a deterrent to aggression is somewhat weak, it has contributed to the air defence of Singapore and Malaysia through the Integrated Air Defence System (IADS). Alliance members acknowledge that the FPDA has been useful in promoting regional stability through the sharing of doctrine and experience by means of regular dialogue at policy-making and operational levels. It also serves as a highly useful confidence-building mechanism between Singapore and Malaysia, despite the problems in their political relations, and enables these countries to hold joint military exercises and training with alliance partners.[22] Thus, Malaysia and Singapore would like to see the FPDA strengthened and expanded. Singapore has proposed a contingency command mechanism within the FPDA which might enable 'FPDA forces to work together, so that should the need ever arise and should the political will ever direct, the FPDA member-countries can combine their military forces together to deal with any threat'.[23] The scope of the FPDA's IADS has been expanded to include the air space in Sabah and Sarawak in East Malaysia.[24] Another possibility is the inclusion of Brunei – which has already been invited as an observer to FPDA chief-of-staff meetings – as a new alliance member. But Indonesia remains opposed to any major new role for the FPDA. Jakarta resents the fact that the alliance was conceived as a deterrent to Indonesia's regional ambitions and sees little need for it in the context of an altered regional security environment.[25]

ASEAN states maintain that their moves to enhance security links with external powers do not imply the abandonment of ZOPFAN, especially as the new relationships do not permit foreign 'bases' but only 'access to local facilities'. But the greater tolerance for such arrangements in the region testifies to the obsolescence of ZOPFAN as a framework for regional security and suggests ASEAN's shift towards a security approach that does not necessarily seek to minimise the involvement of external powers in the region.

Regional dialogues on security
Two factors contributed to the idea that regional dialogues on security issues should be held under the auspices of ASEAN. The first was the attempt by the former foreign secretary of the Philippines, Raul Manglapus, to engage fellow ASEAN members in discussions about 'sharing the burden' of the US military presence in the region. Aiming partly to influence the divisive domestic debate over the US bases, Manglapus sought to persuade fellow ASEAN members that the prospects for a continued US presence in the Philippines would be enhanced if the states were collectively to endorse its contribution as a stabilising factor. But to reach such a decision, ASEAN needed to hold consultations with a view to forging 'a consensus within the region about what it [ASEAN] wants for its security'.[26]

Although the Manglapus initiative was thwarted by the refusal of Indonesia and Malaysia to make a public declaration of their support for the US presence, it helped to desensitise the ASEAN states to the idea of multilateral consultations on security issues. Indeed, Manila held a semi-official conference on regional security in June 1991 where the issue of ASEAN security cooperation was extensively discussed, while Thailand followed with a similar meeting in November 1991.[27] The workshops organised by Indonesia on the Spratly Islands dispute also served to signal ASEAN's willingness to discuss matters affecting regional security in multilateral fora. These discussions paved the way for the decision at the Singapore summit which authorised 'intra-ASEAN dialogues on security cooperation'.

But ASEAN's exposure to the idea of a regional security dialogue was also considerably influenced by developments at the Asia–Pacific level, specifically the proposals from a number of countries for developing new regional security institutions to replace the superpower alliance systems of the Cold War period. These proposals espoused the principle of 'common security' and reflected, at least initially, a desire to apply the lessons of the successful Conference on Security and Cooperation in Europe (CSCE) in Asia.[28] The ball was set rolling by the then Soviet President Mikhail Gorbachev in 1987 who called for a 'Pacific Ocean conference along the [lines of the] Helsinki [CSCE] conference' in his famous speech at Vladivostok in 1987. The Australian Foreign Minister, Gareth Evans, followed in July 1990 by proposing a Conference on Security Cooperation in Asia (CSCA) – 'a future Asian security architecture involving a wholly new institutional process that might be capable of evolving, in Asia just as in Europe, as a framework for addressing and resolving security problems'. Although initially these proposals seemed to envisage an Asia–Pacific version of the CSCE, the analogy was dropped later on the grounds of acknowledged differences in the regional milieu between Europe and Asia. But the essence of the CSCE process could nonetheless be applied to the Asia–Pacific region in the form of the confidence- and security-building measures that had been so successful in reducing Cold War tensions in Europe.[29]

Within ASEAN, these proposals were initially greeted with considerable scepticism and ambivalence. While Malaysia appeared to endorse some of the Soviet proposals for regional confidence-building measures in the superpower strategic context, in general ASEAN leaders echoed the response of the Bush administration which had dubbed the Asian version of the CSCE a 'solution in search of a problem'.[30] Washington viewed any such institution as a threat to its existing alliance system which had proved its worth during the Cold War period. In the words of a Bush administration official: 'While the United States would adjust the form of its security role in the region [in the post-Cold War era], it intends to retain the substance of its role and the bilateral defence relationships which give it structure'.[31]

Echoing the US view, ASEAN leaders argued that the Asia–Pacific was too complex and diverse a region for CSCE-type arrangements. Moreover, if regional and external players were to direct their attention and resources to creating an Asia–Pacific security forum, it might lead ASEAN to 'lose its identity'.[32] A related concern was that a CSCE-type grouping could be used by Western members to press ASEAN on the contentious issue of human rights, which had been a central theme of the CSCE process. ASEAN would clearly and strongly reject any pressure from its Western dialogue partners on human rights or environmental issues as part of their existing consultative agenda.[33]

But while rejecting a formal CSCE-type institution, ASEAN members were more receptive to the use of looser and more consultative mechanisms for promoting an exchange of views within the region on security issues.[34] ASEAN could already boast such fora: the annual meetings between ASEAN foreign ministers and their counterparts from countries which were given the status of official 'dialogue partners' (the ASEAN PMC). The ASEAN PMC, held since 1978, follows the annual AMM, hosted by each member in rotation and itself a forum for security consultations among the ASEAN members.

To ASEAN members, the PMC framework offers several advantages as a forum for dialogue on security within the Asia–Pacific region. First, ASEAN would have a controlling influence over the agenda of discussions and would not risk being sidelined, as might be the case with any new institution. As the former prime minister of Singapore, Lee Kuan Yew, put it: 'In too big and amorphous a club, we will lose our sense of unity and our sense of purpose. But we can do it without losing our separate identity in ASEAN by dialogue with, say, the North Pacific countries and in the South Pacific countries, and then both north and south'.[35] Second, the PMC would enable ASEAN to pursue a more 'inclusive' approach to security in the context of the growing security interdependence between South-east Asia and the wider Pacific theatre. Despite earlier concerns that its regional identity might be diluted by integration into a larger regional process, ASEAN as a grouping could no longer ignore the growing links between subregional (i.e., South-east Asian) security concerns and the developments affecting the role of major Asia–Pacific powers such as the US, Russia, China and Japan. As a Thai scholar argued:

> [ASEAN's] efforts to establish region-wide order in South-east Asia must be related to the larger Asia–Pacific framework of conflict-reduction and cooperation, not only because one needs to recognise the geographical and economic interdependence that exists in this area, but also because one needs to find ways and means of ensuring that extraregional – that is non-South-east Asian – powers' involvements in this region continue to be 'constructive engagements'.[36]

The idea of using the ASEAN PMC as a vehicle for regional security dialogue was also strengthened by the sudden and unexpected support given to it by Japan. Speaking at the AMM in Kuala Lumpur in July 1991, Japanese Foreign Minister Taro Nakayama stated that the ASEAN PMC could be used for 'a process of political discussions designed to improve the sense of security among us'.[37] Although the Japanese proposal received a cool response from the US, it was endorsed, after some initial hesitation, by ASEAN ministers at the meeting.[38] The idea was further developed by the ASEAN-ISIS which, in a report entitled *A Time for Initiative*, proposed that the annual AMMs should be followed by an 'ASEAN PMC-initiated conference to be called "Conference on Stability and Peace in the Asia–Pacific". The meeting, to be held at a suitable retreat . . . for the constructive discussion of Asia–Pacific stability and peace' would include such states as China, Russia, North Korea and Vietnam on a regular basis, while other governments would be invited from time to time depending on the nature of the conference agenda.[39]

While the Singapore summit did not specify which institutions could be used to hold security dialogues at intra-ASEAN and Asia–Pacific levels, the AMM and the ASEAN PMC were clearly meant to play these roles. This was made clear in July 1992 when Manila hosted the first AMM and PMC held since the Singapore summit. At the former, the matter of regional security was 'discussed extensively'.[40] The PMC itself also engaged in what was officially described as an 'Exchange of Views on Political and Security Issues' covering: 'Potential Sources of Tension in the Asia–Pacific Region', including the situation in the Korean peninsula and the South China Sea; 'Trends in Regional Security'; and 'Regional Problems', including Cambodia and Indochinese refugees.[41] In addition, the emphasis on regional security at the Manila meetings was underscored when China, invited to Manila as a guest of ASEAN, offered a pledge not to seek 'hegemony or a sphere of influence' in South-east Asia and not to fill any 'power vacuum' militarily.[42]

While the AMM and PMC complement each other in giving credence to ASEAN's desire to make a significant contribution to a new regional order in South-east Asia and the Asia–Pacific, there are limitations to each framework. The security dialogue within the ASEAN PMC is in some respects a bolder initiative, as it not only signals the deepening of ASEAN regionalism to cover security issues, but also its extension to the wider Asia–Pacific region. But ASEAN clearly is not ready to push this process too far. While the new role for the PMC signalled ASEAN's acknowledgement of the link between subregional security concerns and the changing security order in the Asia–Pacific, a similar broadening of the scope of the Treaty of Amity and Cooperation has been resisted by Indonesia. This was evident in the lead-up to the Singapore summit, when Singapore and Thailand proposed that ASEAN should invite the five permanent members of the UN Security Council to sign the Treaty. But Indonesia resisted the idea, arguing that such a move would engender external interference in the region.[43] This is indicative of the fact that ASEAN is not fully prepared to let other Asia–Pacific powers have a major voice in matters that are more specific to South-east Asia.

The emergence of the ASEAN PMC as a security forum has been endorsed by all the major actors in the region. It also coincided with a perceptible shift in the US attitude towards multilateralism in the Asia–Pacific. This was indicated most specifically in an article in *Foreign Affairs* by the then US Secretary of State James Baker, which expressed support for flexible and *ad hoc* multilateral efforts to deal with specific security problems.[44] The Clinton administration has been more forthcoming in its support for multilateralism, which is identified as one of the ten major goals of the new US policy in Asia.[45] The US shift has added to the appeal of the ASEAN PMC. The fact that this institution has been around for some time enables it to avoid controversy over its structure and function associated with any new institutional framework and makes it more acceptable to countries like the US which are apprehensive about the potential of multilateralism to damage long-established security structures.

But the loose nature of the ASEAN PMC discussions (which are now to be preceded by preparatory meetings at the level of senior officials from PMC countries) intended to minimise such divisions in advance can be an asset as well as a limitation. As a Canadian study correctly points out, the ASEAN PMC is 'both regularized, "low-key", and oriented towards transparency and confidence-building, rather than towards obtaining specific results on currently contentious problems'.[46] As such, the major security issues in the region, such as the Korean peninsula or the territorial dispute between Russia and Japan, would still have to be dealt with through different approaches, including bilateral channels and the more traditional alliance security frameworks.[47] Recent Japanese attitudes towards Asia–Pacific security consultations, while strongly supportive of the ASEAN PMC, nonetheless envisage a 'two-track' approach, one through multilateral discussions on a region-wide basis (the ASEAN PMC being the core), and the other through dialogue among the countries directly involved in a specific conflict.[48]

Moreover, the attraction of the ASEAN PMC has rested partly on ASEAN's own reputation as a regional political institution. But the lessons of its performance in managing inter-state conflict in a subregional context do not necessarily extend to security issues concerning the wider Asia–Pacific region. ASEAN's own role in conflict management was facilitated by the common vulnerability of its member-governments to communist insurgency and the political polarisation of South-east Asia during the Cold War period. The conditions of security cooperation in the wider Asia–Pacific, with its immense economic, political and strategic diversity, are hardly akin to the ASEAN experience. Thus, not surprisingly, some analysts have questioned whether multilateral approaches to security are likely to be more fruitful if undertaken by subregional groupings like ASEAN than by macro-regional ones like the ASEAN PMC.[49] Even if all the major North Pacific actors such as China and North Korea are regularly included in the dialogue, there is still some doubt as to whether the ASEAN PMC would have an appropriate and adequate focus on North-east Asian matters. Interestingly, some proponents of the ASEAN PMC, such as Singapore's Lee Kuan Yew, have conceded the need for a North Pacific equivalent of the PMC to complement ASEAN's own initiative for a regional security dialogue.[50]

Third, the usefulness of the ASEAN PMC is likely to be constrained by disagreement over the common security agenda between ASEAN members and their Western interlocutors. The latter tend to view security in a broader context by incorporating such 'unconventional' threats as environmental degradation, human rights abuses and good government. As noted in Chapter II above, there is substantial disagreement between ASEAN members and Western dialogue partners over these issues, and if the 1992 Manila ASEAN PMC is any indication, ASEAN can be expected to resist Western initiatives on these issues in future PMCs.[51]

The security role of the ASEAN PMC was given a new impetus by the meeting of senior officials from among its members in Singapore in May 1993. This meeting discussed the need and scope for transparency and confidence-building measures within the Asia–Pacific and agreed to expand the scope of PMC security consultations by formally including five new countries: China, Russia, Vietnam, Laos and Papua New Guinea. The 18-member group (to be called the ASEAN Regional Forum), which will convene for the first time in July 1994, represents a further institutionalisation of the Asia–Pacific security dialogue process to be held under the auspices of ASEAN, although the limitations of this process as discussed above still remain.

Managing military competition and collaboration
While ASEAN's role in promoting a security dialogue at the Asia–Pacific level has attracted a good deal of publicity, the evolution of security measures at the intra-ASEAN level is equally crucial to the prospects of regional order in post-Cold War South-east Asia. The intra-ASEAN security consultations sanctioned by the Singapore summit may be viewed as a first step towards a more comprehensive security role for the grouping. But such a role would have to include more concrete and specific measures for greater security and defence cooperation within the grouping, as has been suggested during recent regional security debates.

As noted earlier, in the past, ASEAN states have not viewed defence cooperation as a necessary condition for regional order. On the contrary, such cooperation within the ASEAN framework was rejected for fear that it would provoke greater rivalry with Indochina and undermine ASEAN's quest for regional order. As the end of ASEAN–Indochinese competition removes this barrier, calls for greater ASEAN defence cooperation have surfaced. At the same time, prospects for intra-ASEAN military competition have also been fuelled by a major increase in defence spending and force-modernisation efforts by member-states.

Although some writers have already concluded that post-Cold War South-east Asia is witnessing a regional arms race among ASEAN members,[52] the evidence for this is far from conclusive. Reliable sources of data on defence spending in South-east Asia are scarce and vary widely.[53] Defence expenditure measured in current dollars and exchange rates appears to have increased significantly for all the ASEAN states.[54] But constant dollar figures show a more modest rise (see Table 1). Data from the Stockholm International Peace Research Institute (SIPRI) in 1985 shows that the combined defence expenditure of ASEAN states (except Brunei) in constant US dollars rose from $6,626m in 1987 to $7,121m in 1991, representing an increase of 7.4%. Data from the London-based

Table 1: ASEAN Defence Expenditure Data (constant US$m 1985)

	Brunei		Indonesia		Malaysia		Philippines		Singapore		Thailand	
	IISS	SIPRI	IISS	SIPRI	IISS	SIPRI	IISS	SIPRI	IISS	SIPRI	IISS	SIPRI
1975	n.k.	70	2,069	2,557	719	1,143	760	1,109	642	535	1,012	959
1976	n.k.	123	1,809	3,195	621	1,195	721	1,283	554	647	1,058	1,182
1977	203	124	2,494	3,085	894	1,371	1,121	1,268	678	720	1,230	1,553
1978	196	125	3,126	2,066	1,093	1,152	1,219	826	682	579	1,219	1,278
1979	241	224	2,334	1,971	1,645	1,298	1,082	758	747	582	2,194	1,739
1980	n.k.	234	2,683	2,184	1,760	1,618	792	713	769	653	1,418	1,662
1981	233	224	3,360	2,375	2,405	1,951	942	746	835	747	1,966	1,654
1982	217	242	3,183	2,292	2,365	1,899	1,009	781	824	792	1,711	1,734
1983	276	265	2,701	2,243	2,223	1,468	712	779	1,002	773	1,766	1,858
1984	314	259	2,024	2,205	919	1,108	519	503	939	1,013	1,805	1,989
1985	205	292	2,341	1,936	1,764	977	474	386	1,188	1,151	1,517	2,050
1986	226	326	1,603	1,979	982	1,465	502	424	1,134	1,114	1,524	1,997
1987	179	263	1,704	1,793	1,455	1,286	766	437	1,078	1,125	1,579	1,996
1988	213	287	n.k.	1,717	1,641	1,312	855	476	1,184	1,209	1,573	1,977
1989	n.k.	n.k.	1,570	1,722	1,418	1,362	1,168	645	1,288	1,264	1,493	1,959
1990	n.k.	n.k.	1,776	1,520	1,557	1,380	878	616	1,313	1,305	1,601	2,105
1991	n.k.	n.k.	1,739	1,568	1,670	1,204	843	549	1,518	1,508	1,761	2,292

Sources: International Institute for Strategic Studies, *The Military Balance* (London: Brassey's for the IISS, various years) and Stockholm International Peace Research Institute, *SIPRI Yearbook* (London: Taylor and Francis/Macmillan, various years).

International Institute for Strategic Studies (IISS) shows a higher rate of increase: from $6,582m in 1987 to $7,531m in 1991, or an increase of 14.4%. Furthermore, the rise in defence spending has not been a uniform trend for all the ASEAN countries during this period. For example, SIPRI constant figures for Indonesia and the Philippines show a decline in 1990 compared to the previous year, and for Malaysia a decline in 1991 compared to 1990.

The trend towards increasing defence expenditure in ASEAN is likely to continue for the forseeable future. Indonesia's defence budget for 1993–94 is estimated at $1.95bn, an 18% increase over the past year.[55] In Malaysia, defence and internal security received the biggest increase in the 1991–95 five-year plan, rising from 4.2% of the total allocations to 15.3%.[56] Total defence spending during this period quadrupled to M$6bn from M$1.5bn in the 1986–90 plan.[57] The Philippines has envisaged a ten-year, 10-bn peso programme to modernise its armed forces.[58] On the other hand, defence spending in Thailand can be expected to stabilise in view of the recent decline in the influence of the armed forces in political decision-making.[59] Both Singapore and Brunei are likely to maintain a steady rate of increase in view of recent arms-purchase decisions.

The perception that an arms race might be in progress in South-east Asia is also fuelled by the import of sophisticated weapons by the ASEAN states. Although a detailed description of these purchases is beyond the scope of this study,[60] the common features include procurement of advanced fighter aircraft, airborne early warning capabilities and various naval platforms to create capabilities beyond coastal defence. Brunei is for the first time acquiring fixed-wing combat aircraft with the purchase of *Hawk* jet trainer/strike planes from Britain. The British Aerospace *Hawk* is also being acquired by both Malaysia and Indonesia while the Philippines has settled for a mix of Italian (SIAI-Marchetti S-211), Israeli (*Kfir*) and Czech (*Albatros*) aircraft. Thailand and Singapore are buying additional units of the F-16 fighter aircraft from the US, while Malaysia is seriously considering purchase of the Russian-built MiG-29 '*Fulcrum*' fighters or equivalent aircraft from the US.

Naval force modernisation by ASEAN states includes the acquisition by Brunei and the Philippines of missile-equipped large patrol craft, while larger platforms are being acquired by Malaysia (two guided missile frigates with *Seawolf* point defence missile systems from Britain), Thailand (six Chinese-built frigates and three British-built anti-submarine warfare corvettes) and Indonesia (construction of up to 24 frigates and a class of 1,200-ton corvettes). Indonesia has also bought 39 naval vessels, including 16 corvettes, from the former East German Navy at a cost of $120m. Both Indonesia and Malaysia are considering either the purchase or domestic construction of submarines, while Thailand might soon have the region's first helicopter carrier.

Available evidence suggests that these acquisitions are being driven by a mixture of motives including, but going beyond, intraregional competition. Uncertainties about the military position of extra-regional powers such as the US, Russia, China and Japan are a common motivating factor. Even more important is the combination of the region's economic prosperity and the availability of large quantities of weapons at bargain-basement prices from manufacturers in the West and the former Eastern bloc who are seeking to offset declining sales in their home countries. Beyond this, arms purchases reflect the particular national security concerns of the buyer country. Brunei, Malaysia and the Philippines, all parties to the Spratlys dispute, are developing capabilities with a view to protecting offshore resources. The Philippines has the added imperative of developing a modicum of self-reliance following the departure of US forces from its soil. Although Malaysia's armed forces are shifting from a counter-insurgency to a conventional warfare posture, the air and sea space between Borneo and peninsular Malaysia requires the rapid projection of security forces to suppress internal unrest. Indonesia's force modernisation reflects its position as the largest archipelagic state in the region. Its vast territorial space and the need to exercise control over several of the world's busiest and most strategic sea-lanes in Indonesian national waters has put a premium on air and naval capabilities. Sea-lane security is also of primary concern to Singapore's armed forces, given the island's heavy dependence on seaborne commerce and its status as a regional maritime hub. Intraregional factors, such as prestige and bargaining power, and domestic politics, including the prospect of kickbacks and inter-service rivalry, play a more important part in Thailand's military acquisitions. Although Thailand is periodically embroiled in skirmishes on the Burmese border involving ethnic separatist groups, its armed forces have steadily built up their conventional warfare capabilities through the import of advanced weaponry. Thailand's development of a brown water navy relates to concerns about the naval ambitions of Asian regional powers (although this aspect is clearly overstated by the Thai military), including the need to respond to the growth of Chinese naval power in the South China Sea and that of Indian naval power in the Andaman Sea.

In general, concerns that a regional arms race is in progress in South-east Asia should be seen in the light of a number of factors. First, while the overall spending by ASEAN states has increased, spending in relation to their total GNP has actually declined.[61] Second, no country in South-east Asia seems to be acquiring so-called weapons of mass destruction, including nuclear, biological and chemical weapons and long-range ballistic missiles. (The only possible exceptions could be Vietnam and Burma, which have been accused by US officials of developing a chemical warfare capability.) This sets the region apart from other dangerous hotspots, including the Korean peninsula, South Asia and the Middle East, where the proliferation of 'unconventional' weapons dominates the regional arms races. Third, while territorial disputes and political rivalries between some ASEAN states (especially Singapore and Malaysia or Malaysia and Thailand) undoubtedly form part of the rationale behind force modernisation, such rivalries are not evident in other bilateral relationships. In this context, a host of non-interactive factors are also important in explaining the arms build-up in the region. These include a shared need for greater self-reliance in the wake of superpower retrenchment from the region, as well as perceived threats from competition among extraregional actors such as China, Japan and India. Hence, the interactive dynamic in weapons acquisitions by ASEAN states should not be overstated.

Nonetheless, the current military modernisation programmes could become a threat to regional stability. Even if the ASEAN leaders deny the existence of an arms race in the region,[62] they have acknowledged the fact that the force modernisation efforts by ASEAN states deprive the region of a 'peace dividend'.[63] Moreover, whatever the stated rationale behind these force modernisation efforts, their actual impact on inter-state relations depends on the future regional political climate. As the foreign minister of Australia argues: 'the sort of precautionary worst-case thinking which often characterises strategic planning [in the region] . . . could in turn generate destabilising arms races'.[64]

But arms control and confidence-building measures do not as yet seem to feature in ASEAN's new security approach. Measures to introduce greater transparency in military profiles and limit the spread of sophisticated weapons have almost no precedent in South-east Asia. Proposals by outside experts calling for the creation of a regional body to evaluate defence purchases by ASEAN states and recommend measures towards arms control have been ignored by regional governments.[65]

In recent years, steps have been suggested by some ASEAN leaders to form the basis for a regional arms-control regime. In 1989, Lee Kuan Yew proposed that Singapore and Malaysia should open their key military installations for mutual challenge inspections. The Malaysian defence minister has suggested that ASEAN and its dialogue partners should encourage greater transparency in weapons acquisitions and create a regional arms register based on the UN model so that 'suspicions among each other could be minimised, and managed'.[66] But neither of these proposals has been translated into action.

On the other hand, arguments that arms control may not be a necessary element of regional order in South-east Asia point not only to the existing consensus against the use of force in the region, but also to the role of existing forms of security cooperation within ASEAN in promoting confidence-building. Singapore's defence minister asserted that 'strong ties' among defence heads in ASEAN has helped to 'foster greater mutual confidence and trust',[67] while bilateral military exercises among ASEAN states have been cited as helping to 'build links with . . . neighbours, overcome suspicions and promote cooperation'.[68]

In this context, proposals for a multilateral defence arrangement within ASEAN have been somewhat more fashionable to regional policy-makers than those relating to arms control. Such an arrangement is seen by its advocates as a necessary complement to regional order, both in terms of its expected utility in reinforcing the tradition of cooperation that already binds ASEAN states, and its potential for instilling a greater degree of confidence among members in the face of mutually perceived external threats.

Most proposals for an ASEAN-wide defence arrangement have lacked precise definition. Two recent examples include the call for an ASEAN 'defence community' made by the then foreign minister of Malaysia, Abu Hasan Omar, in 1989,[69] and the idea of an ASEAN military pact mooted by the National Security Adviser of the Philippines in 1991.[70] Neither proposal received the full official backing of the respective governments and in the case of Malaysia, the government appeared to distance itself from it.[71]

The consensus against a military pact developed since ASEAN's inception remains. Indonesia's former defence chief, General Try Sutrisno, contended that 'without a military pact . . . [the ASEAN states] can cooperate more flexibly'.[72] The former chief of staff of Malaysia argued that bilateral cooperation still remains preferable to a pact because 'it allows any ASEAN partner to decide the type, time and scale of aid it requires or can provide' and ensures that 'the question of national independence and sovereignty [of members] is unaffected by the decision of others as in the case of an alliance where members can invoke the terms of the treaty and interfere in the affairs of another partner'.[73] This position was confirmed by the preparatory meeting of ASEAN Foreign and Economic Ministers before the Singapore summit:

> ASEAN is not and should not become a military alliance. Each member-country must always assume primary responsibility for its own defence and security.[74]

It may be argued, despite the rejection of a formal defence pact, that a *de facto* 'defence community' already exists within ASEAN, based on a 'spider-web' network of defence links undertaken bilaterally by the ASEAN states. The foundation of these ties was laid in the 1970s when, as discussed in Chapter II, bilateral border security agreements and intelligence-sharing were developed to combat the problem of insurgency. Since the 1980s, the focus of cooperation has broadened to include joint conventional warfare exercises, exchanges of training facilities and cooperation on defence production. But does such cooperation testify to the notion of a defence community?

Table 2: Bilateral Military Exercises in ASEAN

Countries Involved	Name of Exercise	Year Started	Frequency
Indonesia/ Malaysia (Army)	Kekar Malindo/ Tatar Malindo/ Kripura Malindo	1977 1981 1981	Annual Intermittent Intermittent
Indonesia/ Malaysia (Air)	Elang Malindo	1975	Annual
Indonesia/ Malaysia (Navy)	Malindo Jaya	1973	Annual(?)
Indonesia/ Malaysia (all services)	Darsasa Malindo	1982	Intermittent
Indonesia/ Singapore (Army)	Safakar Indopura	1989	Annual
Indonesia/ Singapore (Air)	Elang Indopura	1980	Annual
Indonesia/ Singapore (Navy)	Englek	1974	Biennial
Indonesia/ Thailand (Air)	Elang Thainesia	1981	Annual
Indonesia/ Thailand (Navy)	Sea Garuda	1975(?)	Intermittent
Indonesia/ Philippines (Navy)	Philindo/ Corpatphilindo	1972	Intermittent
Malaysia/ Singapore (Army)	Semangat Bersatu	1989	Annual
Malaysia/ Singapore (Navy)	Malapura	1984	Annual
Malaysia/ Thailand (Air)	Air Thamal	1981	Annual
Malaysia/ Thailand (Navy)	Thalay	1980	Intermittent(?)
Malaysia/ Brunei (Navy)	Hornbill (and others)	1981(?)	Intermittent
Singapore/ Thailand (Air)	Sing-Siam	1981(?)	Intermittent
Singapore/ Thailand (Navy)	Thai-Sing	1983	Annual

Singapore/ Philippines (Army)	Anoa-Singa	1993	Annual(?)
Singapore/ Brunei (Navy)	Pelican	1979	Annual
Singapore/ Brunei (Army)	Termite/ Flaming Arrow	1985	Annual

Sources: *New Straits Times*, 21 August 1980, 21 February 1981, 30 August 1983, 17 November 1983, 9 May 1984; *The Star*, 18 November 1982, 20 August 1983, 20 November 1986, 17 August 1988, 26 May 1989; Donald Weatherbee, 'ASEAN Security Cooperation and the South China Sea', paper presented to the Pacific Forum Symposium, 'National Threat Perceptions in East-Asia Pacific', Waikoloa, Hawaii, 6–8 February 1982; personal interviews in Kuala Lumpur, Malaysia, 16 August 1989; *Asian Defence Journal*, no. 5, 1976, p. 26, and January 1988, p. 18; *Indonesia Observer*, 10 August 1989; *The Straits Times*, 13 June 1973, 28 January 1975, 18 August 1983, 3 August 1989, 16 December 1989, 6 July 1990; *Pioneer*, no. 74, May 1984, no. 82, August 1984, no. 84, October 1984, no. 109, November 1986, no. 120, October 1987, no. 129, July 1988, no. 141, July 1989; *Bangkok Post*, 7 January 1982; *China News*, 4 November 1975; personal interview with the Defence Attaché of the Philippines, Jakarta, 10 August 1989; *Sunday Times* (Singapore), 21 May 1989; B. A. Hamzah, 'ASEAN Military Cooperation Without Pact or Threat', *Asia Pacific Community*, no. 22, Autumn 1983, pp. 42–43; K. U. Menon, 'A Six-Power Defence Arrangement in Southeast Asia', *Contemporary Southeast Asia*, vol. 10, no. 3, December 1988, p. 314; *Asia–Pacific Defence Reporter*, June–July 1992, p. 26.

To begin with, bilateral defence links within ASEAN are not uniformly developed. As Table 2 indicates, the majority of bilateral exercises take place between three countries: Indonesia, Malaysia and Singapore. A good part of the recent expansion of defence links in ASEAN has also involved these three states. Examples include the launching of the *Semangat Bersatu* army exercises between Singapore and Malaysia in 1989, the *Safakar Indopura* army exercise between Singapore and Indonesia in 1989, the *Darsasa Malindo* all-services exercise between Malaysia and Indonesia in 1982, and the opening of a 10,850-hectare air weapons testing range in Siabu, Sumatra, in March 1989, jointly developed by Indonesia and Singapore.[75] In February 1992, Indonesia and Malaysia signed a memorandum of understanding to expand their cooperation in joint exercises, exchange of personnel and logistics.[76] Indeed, the rapid proliferation of defence ties among Singapore, Malaysia and Indonesia led the former foreign minister of Indonesia, Mochtar Kusumaatmadja, to propose the creation of a trilateral defence arrangement involving the three states as a replacement for the FPDA,[77] although this does not seem politically feasible in view of the unease felt by Malaysia over the growing bilateral military links between Singapore and Indonesia. Kuala Lumpur has felt that the growing security ties between Indonesia and Singapore could be at the expense of Malaysian–Indonesian relations,[78] and that

Singapore's interest in developing close security ties with Indonesia could partly be due to its strategy of using the latter as a counterweight to Malaysian pressure.[79]

Even outside the trilateral core, some defence relations within ASEAN are stronger and more developed than others. A particularly close relationship obtains between Singapore and Brunei. Brunei has sought Singapore's help 'in matters relating to defence technology, personnel and logistics management'.[80] In return, Singapore's army training facilities in Brunei have been described as the 'most valuable single facility [for the Singapore Armed Forces] which will be difficult to duplicate elsewhere'.[81] Singapore has also maintained close ties with Thailand by maintaining two army camps within Thai territory,[82] while Thailand sends its troops to Singapore for commando training. On the other hand, defence relations between Malaysia and Brunei remain low-key due to strained political ties between the two countries (including the latter's suspicions of Malaysian interference in its domestic affairs), although the two countries recently signed a memorandum of understanding providing for joint exercises and cooperation in exchange for personnel and logistics.[83] The Sabah dispute has prevented the development of any cooperation between the armed forces of Malaysia and the Philippines. In fact, Manila's bilateral defence links with all its ASEAN neighbours have been rather limited in scope, the important exception being the use of US military bases in the Philippines (especially the Clark air base and the Crow Valley Weapon Testing Range) by Singapore and Thai air forces. But this has ended with the departure of US forces from the Philippines which may explain Manila's recent enthusiasm for defence cooperation within ASEAN.

Another barrier to an ASEAN defence community can be found in the joint production of defence equipment. In 1989, the Philippines advocated that ASEAN states should look for 'common sourcing ... which might be beneficial to the Philippines with regard to the production of defence supplies and materials'.[84] A similar suggestion, calling for cooperation in the production of weapons to be traded within the region, has also been made by Thailand.[85] In fact, Thailand and Singapore have already arranged to co-produce a range of small arms (including 40mm rocket-propelled grenade launchers) which could also be available for export.[86] Similarly, Malaysia and Indonesia signed an agreement in February 1992 to collaborate on the developments of their defence industries.[87] But Singapore has not been as responsive to similar co-production arrangements with Malaysia.[88] As the region's most advanced arms producer, Singapore is sceptical of the possibility of an ASEAN arms industry. In Singapore's view, each ASEAN country has to have its own approach to strategic industry as the priorities of individual countries are different in key areas of military engineering and weapons systems.[89]

A similar problem affects proposals calling for greater standardisation of weapons among the ASEAN states. Although a certain degree of standardisation is evident, especially in the area of combat aircraft (F-5, A-4, F-16 and the British Aerospace *Hawk*), ground forces equipment (*Scorpion* light tanks and V-150 *Commando* personnel carriers) and a range of advanced missile systems (*Rapier*, *Exocet* and *Sidewinder*), this is not due to any conscious design.[90] In none of the cases has joint procurement been attempted to save costs, although such opportunities must have been present (especially in the case of combat aircraft such as the F-16).[91] The possibility of greater coordination in the future faces obstacles such as the different levels of defence spending among ASEAN countries and the divergent strategic priorities of their armed forces based on peculiarities in geography, territorial depth and doctrine.[92]

Furthermore, despite the regular conduct of joint exercises and training, the armed forces of the ASEAN states have not developed a significant degree of inter-operability and integration. Differences in defence doctrines and language, as well as variances in training procedures and logistics systems, limit the benefits to be derived from joint exercises and undermine the possibility of mutual support in contingencies.[93] Contrast, for example, Singapore's emphasis on forward defence with Indonesia's emphasis on 'defence-in-depth', or Thailand's preoccupation (at least until recently) with land-based threats from the north with Malaysia's focus on maritime security and the safety of the sea-lanes of communication between its peninsular and island halves. The armed forces of the Philippines face the difficult task of catching up with their ASEAN counterparts in switching to a conventional warfare orientation, although the declining communist insurgency and the removal of the US military umbrella has created an urgent need for it.

Given the difficulties facing the closer integration of weapon systems and doctrines within ASEAN, more limited measures for defence policy coordination have been mooted. The chief of the armed forces of the Philippines, General Lisandro Abadia, proposed the idea of an ASEAN consultative mechanism to address security-related issues such as drug-trafficking and sea-lane security.[94] The establishment of an ASEAN defence committee at the level of senior officers remains a possibility, although the ASEAN summit in Singapore rejected a proposal for such a forum.[95]

This may seem at odds with the grouping's overall objective of greater security autonomy in view of the possibility that the heightened prospects for intra-ASEAN military competition caused by increased defence spending and force modernisation might be offset to some degree by a corresponding level of increase in bilateral and multilateral military cooperation. The state of military relations within the grouping, in their competitive as well as collaborative dimensions, has become important enough to require ASEAN's collective attention, and managing these issues within the ASEAN framework need not contravene its decision not to become a military alliance.

CONCLUSION

The ASEAN Post-Ministerial Conference in July 1993 agreed to set up the ASEAN Regional Forum – a new framework for the ASEAN-PMC participants to begin talking about 'preventive diplomacy' after the end of the Cold War. But unless ASEAN and other interested parties move beyond the dialogue of a dining club and begin focusing on concrete action, the challenges to regional security will go unmet. On one level, the challenge is one of several dimensions. On one level, it consists of simply maintaining intramural cohesion in the absence of a common security threat or unifying concern (such as the Cambodian conflict). On another level, the challenge is one of responding to new threats to regional stability that have replaced Cold War geopolitics. Yet another aspect of ASEAN's post-Cold War security dilemma is the need to broaden its horizons beyond the hitherto narrow subregional focus. The task of integrating the reform-minded Indochinese countries under its auspices and responding to new ideas about regional order in the wider Asia–Pacific milieu has presented ASEAN with difficult choices which it can neither ignore nor resolve in quick, easy steps.

In confronting the challenges of the 1990s, ASEAN has to contend with the loss – with the end of bipolarity – of a familiar, if not fool-proof, structure of regional security. What is more, the early optimism for post-Cold War regional stability generated by the end of the US–Soviet and Sino-Soviet rivalries has been substantially eroded. While the possibility of a major armed international conflict in South-east Asia may seem remote at the moment, strategic uncertainties and potential flashpoints abound. Certainly, no ASEAN leader is sanguine about the changing regional balance of power, even if none can point to any clear external threat to regional stability.

While the collapse of communism coincided with the decline of one of the major threats to the regime survival of the ASEAN states, namely communist insurgency, this may have had the paradoxical effect of eroding a principal basis of unity within the grouping. Moreover, the threat of a violent challenge to ASEAN regimes does not end with communist insurrection. The ostensible signs of a decline in the military's influence over the political process in Indonesia, the Philippines and Thailand may prove temporary, and regime stability in all three countries will continue to be vulnerable to civil–military tensions. Similarly, domestic order in Malaysia and Indonesia remains subject to another long-standing problem, the status of the overseas Chinese minority in these societies. High economic growth rates may have muted poltical and racial strife within ASEAN societies, but this happy situation remains subject to shifts in the global economy which might impose sudden hardship on the developing economies in the region.

The issues of political participation and human rights are relatively new items on the international relations agenda of the ASEAN states, but have important implications for the grouping's political and security role in the post-Cold War era. Some ASEAN regimes are already finding it increasingly difficult to cope with the demands for greater openness from sections of their populations within the existing authoritarian political structures. Thus political violence stemming from campaigns for greater political participation and leadership change remains a possibility in some states, including Indonesia. At the same time, Western pressures regarding human rights abuses related to the suppression of ethnic and religious-based rebellions might encourage these groups and undermine the concerned ASEAN governments' ability to deal with such threats to domestic order. Western criticism of Indonesia's handling of its separatist movements in Aceh and East Timor is illustrative of the pressures facing an ASEAN regime on the human rights front.

The rapid expansion of economic and diplomatic ties between ASEAN members and Vietnam and Laos is suggestive of progress towards the professed goal of 'one South-east Asia'. But this process involves obstacles and dilemmas. ASEAN has already faced intramural competition over Indochinese markets. Thai efforts to create a special relationship with Indochina and Burma, if pursued to the extreme, could lead to the *de facto* polarisation of South-east Asia into continental and maritime spheres. In addition, Vietnam's attempt to seek ASEAN backing against Chinese pressure would also have a divisive impact on intra-ASEAN cohesion, as some members are likely to be more sympathetic to Hanoi's predicament than others. In the meantime, Vietnam and several ASEAN members remain embroiled in territorial disputes which have not been brought closer to solution despite the new-found spirit of cooperation. In this context, the prospects for a security partnership between ASEAN and Vietnam in encountering extraregional powers like China seem rather unrealistic.

Territorial disputes involving maritime boundaries and EEZs pose another set of challenges to the post-Cold War regional order in South-east Asia. These issues are, however, yet to put significant strain on bilateral relations, for example those between Singapore and Malaysia or Malaysia and Indonesia, and no ASEAN country seriously envisages the use of force to pursue its territorial claims. But these claims are a factor underlying the military modernisation programmes of ASEAN states and undermine its credibility as a regional security community at a time when intramural cohesion is no longer served by issues like communism or Cambodia. Indeed, recent warnings by military commanders in Indonesia and Thailand about the possibility of low-intensity conflicts in post-Cold War South-east Asia are indicative of regional apprehensions about unresolved territorial issues.

A similar observation can be made about territorial disputes in the South China Sea. Here, too, the prospect of conflict can be overstated. There are powerful reasons why the larger states involved in the disputes – China, Vietnam, Malaysia and the Philippines – would exercise restraint in pursuing their claims. But the issue has already been included in the military calculations of the regional actors, explaining, at least partly, the ambitious military modernisation programmes undertaken by some ASEAN states. The Spratly Islands issue is also intimately linked to regional concerns about the post-Cold War role of China. While China's modernising military establishment is still deficient in its power-projection capabilities, it is already seen by ASEAN states as potentially the most significant challenge to the regional balance of power.

While threats to regional order from intraregional conflicts remain, in South-east Asia, a more alarming scenario revolves around the prospective role of Asian regional powers in the post-Cold War environment. Sober analysis might indicate that a sudden attempt by any of the so-called regional powers to fill the void left by superpower retrenchment is highly unlikely. The would-be contenders, such as China, Japan or India, lack either the military capability and/or the political will to make such a move in the near term. The relative position of regional powers will evolve gradually and will be subject to other influences, such as the role of the US, domestic developments in both China and Russia and the military and diplomatic policies of regional actors, including ASEAN members.

Nonetheless, the prospect and implications of a regional power vacuum are increasingly important to the security thinking of ASEAN states, driven largely by questions about the future of the US military presence in the region. Despite numerous assurances from US policy-makers regarding its determination to remain the principal Pacific military power, force-structure adjustments currently envisaged have already contributed to a climate of acute strategic uncertainty in the minds of ASEAN security planners. While a common feeling of strategic uncertainty can be a unifying factor for the Association, similar to a commonly perceived external threat, it may also exacerbate existing differences in threat perceptions within the grouping. (These differences are already sharpened by suspicions harboured by Malaysia and Indonesia over closer economic and political relations between Singapore and China.) Strategic uncertainty is also a factor, although not necessarily the most important one, behind the regional arms build-up which, unless managed through a system of greater transparency and confidence-building measures, could be perceived as mutually threatening in an intra-ASEAN context.

Against this backdrop, the prospect of a post-Cold War regional order in South-east Asia would seem to revolve around the question of whether ASEAN itself can help fill the security gap by mobilising its collective diplomatic, political and military resources. Of these, the role of collective military means is easier to dismiss. The ASEAN members' reluctance to engage in multilateral defence cooperation remains unchanged. Indeed, *rapprochement* with Vietnam, stronger security links with the US and the diplomatic engagement of extraregional powers to explore the possibility of a multilateral security framework might have further eroded the rationale for an ASEAN military pact. Although bilateral defence links within the grouping may be strengthened, and regular meetings between its security officials agreed upon, this would hardly match the importance of national defence capabilities and extraregional security links in the ASEAN states' security postures. Neither can it serve as a significant component of the grouping's framework for regional order in the post-Cold War era.

A more realistic course for ASEAN is to strive, with the help of new political and diplomatic measures, towards a multilateral security framework which would strengthen its existing role in conflict-reduction within South-east Asia and constrain the role of major Asian and extraregional actors in the regional security environment. After some initial hesitation, ASEAN has come to recognise and accept the need for such a framework covering the larger Asia–Pacific region. But its evolution has not proceeded much beyond sponsorship of academic and semi-official seminars and consultations. There is no clear consensus within ASEAN on the actual shape of a new multilateral security institution which might eventually result from the loose process of consultations already provided by the ASEAN PMC. Some members continue to harbour misgivings that a new institution would overshadow ASEAN's own role in regional security (Indonesia), or undermine the relevance of the US-sponsored bilateral alliances which must be maintained in the interest of regional stability (Singapore).

In this context, the appeal of Asia–Pacific multilateralism as an approach to regional order in South-east Asia has been a double-edged instrument for ASEAN. On the one hand, it presents the grouping with an unprecedented opportunity to extend the norms and principles developed in its subregional context to a wider regional milieu. But this wider milieu is also a far more complex strategic setting in which regional order would require capabilities and resources beyond those that ASEAN-led institutions (such as the PMC) can provide. Thus, by projecting a role in the wider Asia–Pacific context, ASEAN would risk its regional managerial function being overshadowed by larger, more powerful regional actors, as has already happened in the case of Cambodia. Moreover, its approach to political and security issues in their broader non-military dimensions is not fully compatible with those of the Western participants, as has been seen over the issues of human rights and democratisation. In a related vein, ASEAN can only muster limited resources and influence in managing broader regional conflicts such as the Spratly Islands dispute or the delicate and dangerous situation in the Korean peninsula.

Neither can multilateralism be a substitute for old-fashioned balance-of-power mechanisms which, in the ASEAN states' view, remain critical to the prospects for regional order in the post-Cold War era. This leads to an irony in the grouping's post-Cold War security posture as it relates to the issue of multilateralism. While the conditions for realising ASEAN's existing multilateral security frameworks, such as ZOPFAN and SEANWFZ, have been made favourable by superpower retrenchment, these frameworks are also deemed less relevant in a new geopolitical climate in which regional powers such as China and Japan are viewed as the principal challengers to regional stability. These powers cannot be trusted to guarantee the viability of a security regime like ZOPFAN. This realisation has led ASEAN states virtually to abandon ZOPFAN and seek ever-closer security ties with the US, a move which has been helped by the removal, with the demise of superpower competition, of some of the political constraints on an explicit US–ASEAN security relationship.

Thus, despite an ostensible interest in exploring the ideas being proposed for common and cooperative security in the Asia–Pacific region, the ASEAN states' preferred approach to regional order seems to lie in the maintenance of a regional balance of power, underpinned by the superior and forward-deployed military resources of the US and capable of deterring Chinese and Japanese regional ambitions. But such a security system is also one over which weak local actors such as the ASEAN members can have little control. Herein lies a final contradiction in the Association's post-Cold War security posture. Its desire to assume a managerial role in regional order is, and would remain, circumscribed by shifts in the regional balance of power which are essentially externally driven. Such a security structure not only deprives ASEAN of any ability to insulate the region from outside intervention and influence, but also gives it only a limited ability to constrain, through dialogue and consultations, the engagement of external powers so as to make it conform to its own security needs.

Notes

Introduction

[1] *Singapore Declaration of 1992*, ASEAN Heads of Government Meeting, Singapore, 27–28 January 1992, Press Release, p. 2.
[2] These issues are extensively dealt with in a number of excellent studies on ASEAN's security role. See especially, Arnfinn Jorgensen-Dahl, *Regional Organization and Order in Southeast Asia* (London: Macmillan, 1982); Sheldon Simon, *The ASEAN States and Regional Security* (Stanford, CA: Hoover Institution Press, 1982); Michael Leifer, *ASEAN and the Security of Southeast Asia* (London: Routledge, 1989).
[3] I acknowledge the help of Dr Gerald Segal in suggesting some of the specific questions and issues addressed in this study.

Chapter I

[1] For an excellent discussion of continuity and change in the security environment of South-east Asia, see Muthiah Alagappa, 'The Dynamics of International Security in Southeast Asia: Change and Continuity', *Australian Journal of International Affairs*, vol. 45, no. 1, May 1991.
[2] The best analysis of the Cold War regional order in South-east Asia is found in Michael Leifer, *Conflict and Regional Order in South-east Asia*, Adelphi Paper 162 (London: Brassey's for the IISS, 1980). See also his earlier work, *Foreign Affairs of the New States* (Melbourne: Longman, 1974).
[3] Amitav Acharya, 'Regionalism and Regime Security in the Third World: Comparing the Origins of ASEAN and the GCC', in Brian L. Job (ed.), *The Insecurity Dilemma: National Security of Third World States* (Boulder, CO: Lynne Reiner, 1992).
[4] The difference between the two conceptions of regional security in South-east Asia is explored in Amitav Acharya, 'The Association of Southeast Asian Nations: "Security Community" or "Defence Community"', *Pacific Affairs*, vol. 62, no. 2, Summer 1991, pp. 159–78.
[5] For a detailed assessment of the Cambodian peace process during this period, see Amitav Acharya, Pierre Lizée and Soropong Peou, *Cambodia: The 1989 Paris Peace Conference* (New York: Kraus International, 1991).
[6] The concept of the 'security community' was developed in Karl Deutsch, *et al.*, *Political Community in the North Atlantic Area* (Princeton, NJ: Princeton University Press, 1957). Sheldon Simon argues that ASEAN 'may be a security community in the sense that no member would seriously consider the use of force against another to settle disputes'. See 'The Regionalization of Defence in Southeast Asia', *Pacific Review*, vol. 5, no. 2, 1992, p. 122.
[7] 'A New Call for Unity', *Asiaweek*, 22 October 1982.
[8] *Jakarta Post*, 9 September 1989.
[9] It is interesting that the Russian Ambassador to Hanoi has indicated Moscow's desire to continue using Cam Ranh Bay under a new agreement. Although he confirmed the presence of 1,000 Russian servicemen at Cam Ranh, Vietnamese sources have put the figure at around 400 servicemen and family members. See *The Straits Times*, 28 August 1992, p. 4.
[10] In addition to the 11% reduction from an original strength of 135,000 personnel (including 25,000 on board ships) envisaged under EASI-I, 8,100 personnel have been withdrawn from the Philippines. A further reduction of about 10% is planned for the second phase of EASI (1993–95). See Susumu Awanohara, 'America's Easi Options', *Far Eastern Economic Review*, 3 September 1992, p. 23.
[11] 'Too Committed to Withdraw from Asia', interview with Admiral Charles Larson, Commander-in-Chief, US

Pacific Command, *Asia–Pacific Defence Reporter*, vol. 19, nos 2/3, August–September 1992, p. 33.
[12] William T. Pendley, 'US Security Strategy in East Asia for the 1990s', *Strategic Review*, vol. 20, no. 3, Summer 1992, pp. 12–13. Pendley served as Deputy Assistant Secretary of State for East Asia and Pacific Affairs under the Bush administration.
[13] The former foreign minister of Indonesia, Mochtar Kusumaatmadja, refers to these countries as 'the emerging powers in Asia with hegemonistic ambitions'. See 'Some Thoughts on ASEAN Security Cooperation: An Indonesian Perspective', *Contemporary Southeast Asia*, vol. 12, no. 3, December 1990, p. 168.
[14] *The Straits Times*, 10 February 1990.
[15] Malaysia's former chief of the armed forces, General Hashim Mohammed Ali, noted in March 1992 that while India was constrained by domestic problems and Japan by constitutional limitations, China continued to increase its defence spending and had threatened the use of force to support its territorial claims in the South China Sea. See *The Sunday Times* (Singapore), 29 March 1992. Indonesia's armed forces commander, General Try Sutrisno, also expressed similar concerns about China. See *The Straits Times*, 6 October 1992.
[16] 'Live and Let Live', *Far Eastern Economic Review*, 11 July 1991, p. 13.
[17] Lee Kuan Yew in *The Straits Times* (weekly overseas edition), 14 November 1992, p. 24.
[18] Text of statement by Datuk Abdullah Ahmad Badawi, Malaysian Minister for Foreign Affairs, at the Paris Peace Conference on Cambodia, 23 October 1991, p. 2.
[19] Thai Prime Minister Anand Panyarachun, *The Straits Times*, 25 June 1991.
[20] Text of statement by Ali Alatas, Indonesian Minister for Foreign Affairs and Co-Chairman of the Paris Peace Conference on Cambodia, 23 October 1991, p. 4.
[21] See Donald Weatherbee, *ASEAN After Cambodia: The Reordering of Southeast Asia*, Asian Update Series (New York: Asia Society, June 1989), pp. 8–9.
[22] Leszek Buszynski, 'Declining Superpowers: The Impact on ASEAN', *Pacific Review*, vol. 3, no. 3, 1990, p. 258.
[23] Chin Kin Wah, 'Changing Global Trends and Their Effects on the Asia–Pacific', *Contemporary Southeast Asia*, vol. 13, no. 1, June 1991, p. 13.
[24] *The Straits Times*, 24 August 1992, p. 12.
[25] *International Herald Tribune (IHT)*, 29 October 1992.
[26] Text of speech by Foreign Minister Wong Kan Seng at the Defence Asia '89 conference on 'Towards Greater ASEAN Military and Security Cooperation: Issues and Prospects', Singapore, 22–25 March 1989, 24 March 1989.
[27] Jusuf Wanandi, 'Towards a New Regional Order for ASEAN', paper presented to the symposium on 'The Changing Role of the United Nations in Conflict Resolution and Peacekeeping', sponsored jointly by the United Nations Department of Public Information and the Institute of Policy Studies, Singapore, 13–15 March 1991, p. 4.

Chapter II

[1] For a discussion, see Franklin B. Weinstein, 'The Meaning of National Security in Southeast Asia', *Bulletin of Atomic Scientists*, vol. 34, no. 9, November 1978, pp. 20–28.
[2] This point is made, among others, by Mochtar Kusumaatmadja. According to him, internal conflicts need not threaten regional stability, but the same cannot be said about the prospects for international conflict, including territorial conflicts and the ambitions of regional powers such as China, Japan and India. See 'Some Thoughts on ASEAN

Security Cooperation', pp. 161–71.
[3] *The Straits Times* (weekly overseas edition), 9 December 1989.
[4] Paisal Sricharatchanya, 'Seeking Total Victory', *Far Eastern Economic Review*, 29 October 1987, p. 22; *The Straits Times*, 27 October 1988; John McBeth, 'Out in the Woods', *Far Eastern Economic Review*, 11 January 1990, p. 20.
[5] *The Straits Times* (weekly overseas edition), 9 December 1989.
[6] *The Straits Times*, 28 November 1988.
[7] *Ibid.*, 7 January 1992.
[8] *Ibid.*, 28 November 1988, p. 12; Foreign Broadcast Information Service (FBIS) EAS-92-037, 25 February 1992, p. 59.
[9] Napoleon Y. Navarro, 'The Philippines in 1991: Anticipating the Elections', in *Southeast Asian Affairs 1991* (Singapore: Institute of Southeast Asian Studies, 1992), p. 266.
[10] Sukhumbhand Paribatra and Chai-Anan Samudavanija, 'Internal Dimensions of Regional Security in Southeast Asia', in Mohammed Ayoob (ed.), *Regional Security in the Third World* (London: Croom Helm, 1986), pp. 61–62.
[11] Tai Ming Cheung, 'Elusive Threat', *Far Eastern Economic Review*, 22 April 1993, p. 26.
[12] Michael Leifer, *Dilemmas of Statehood in Southeast Asia* (Singapore: Asia Pacific Press, 1972), p. 37.
[13] This explanation of separatism in South-east Asia, perhaps the most sophisticated to date, can be found in David Brown, 'From Peripheral Communities to Ethnic Nations: Separatism in Southeast Asia', *Pacific Affairs*, vol. 61, no. 1, Spring 1988, pp. 51–77.
[14] *The Straits Times*, 13 May 1993, p. 16.
[15] *Ibid.*
[16] Tan Lian Choo, 'Personality Politics in Thailand', in *Southeast Asian Affairs 1991*, p. 289.
[17] Max Lane, 'The Philippines 1990: Political Stalemate and Persisting Instability', in *ibid.*, p. 239.
[18] Tan Lian Choo, 'Personality Politics in Thailand', p. 286.
[19] Hussin Mutalib, 'Islamic Revivalism in ASEAN States', *Asian Survey*, vol. 30, no. 9, September 1990, pp. 877–91.
[20] See Tilak Doshi, 'Brunei: The Steady State', in *Southeast Asian Affairs 1991*, pp. 76–77.
[21] Michael Vatikiotis, *Indonesian Politics Under Suharto* (London: Routledge, 1993), p. 128.
[22] Chan Heng Chee, 'Political Stability in Southeast Asia', paper presented to the seminar on 'Trends and Perspectives in ASEAN', organised by the Institute of Southeast Asian Studies, Singapore, 1–3 February 1982, p. 11.
[23] See Fred Riggs, *Thailand: The Modernization of a Bureaucratic Polity* (Honolulu, HI: East–West Center Press, 1966); see also John L.S. Girling, *The Bureaucratic Polity in Modernising Societies: Similarities, Differences and Prospects in the ASEAN Region* (Singapore: Institute of Southeast Asian Studies, 1981).
[24] The following is a good definition of the 'trickle-down effect': 'Development strategies generally chosen by non-Communist Southeast Asian governments are aimed at bringing about rapid economic growth with focus on urban-based industrial promotion and utilization of advanced technology in an atmosphere of free enterprise. The underlying assumption is that sooner or later there will be "trickle-down effects" and any maladjustments in terms of distribution will automatically be corrected. In that eventuality equity in terms of equal shares will not be achieved, but everyone's demands and requirements will be "satisfied" and there will be further incentive to work for another round of growth and trickle-down effects'. Paribatra and Samudavanija, 'Internal Dimensions of Regional Security in Southeast Asia', p. 67.
[25] Harold Crouch, 'Malaysia: Neither

Authoritarian, Nor Democratic', in Kevin Hewison, Richard Robison and Garry Rodan (eds), *Southeast Asia in the 1990s: Authoritarianism, Democracy and Capitalism* (Sydney: Allen and Unwin, 1993), p. 142.

[26] Chan Heng Chee, 'Democracy: Evolution and Implementation: An Asian Perspective', paper presented at the 'Conference on Asian and American Perspectives on Capitalism and Democracy', Singapore, 28–30 January 1993, p. 11.

[27] Michael Leifer, 'The Paradox of ASEAN: A Security Organisation without the Structure of an Alliance', *Round Table*, vol. 68, no. 271, July 1978, p. 268.

[28] These agreements are: the Thai–Malaysia Police Frontier Agreement (1949); the Agreement on Border Operations Against Communist Terrorists Between the Government of Thailand and the Government of the Federation of Malay (1959); the Agreement Between the Government of Thailand and the Government of Malaysia on Border Cooperation (1965 and 1970); and the Agreement Between the Government of Malaysia and the Government of Thailand on Border Cooperation (1977). See Roslan Kuntom, 'Bilateral Border Security Cooperation Between Malaysia and Thailand', paper presented to the First Annual Thailand–Malaysia Colloquium, Bangkok, 2–3 September, 1987, pp. 2–3.

[29] Tunku Abdul Rahman, 'Indonesian Peace Mission', *The Star*, 15 August 1983.

[30] 'Malaysia/Indonesia Security Arrangements', *Foreign Affairs Malaysia*, vol. 5, no. 2, June 1972, pp. 63–65.

[31] *New Straits Times*, 8 December 1981.

[32] Michael Richardson, 'ASEAN Extends Its Military Ties', *Pacific Defence Reporter*, November 1982, p. 55.

[33] *The Straits Times*, 23 December 1976.

[34] *The New Nation*, 16 February 1977.

[35] *The Straits Times*, 23 September 1978.

[36] Michael Vatikiotis, 'Dollar Democracy', *Far Eastern Economic Review*, 26 September 1991, p. 35.

[37] *New Straits Times*, 31 October 1991.

[38] 'Private Pressure', *Far Eastern Economic Review*, 13 February 1992, p. 9.

[39] *The Straits Times*, 23 July 1991.

[40] This point is made by a senior Singapore Foreign Ministry official. See Kishore Mahbubani, 'The West and the Rest', *The National Interest*, no. 28, Summer 1992, p. 9.

[41] *The Environment and Human Rights in International Relations* (Jakarta: ASEAN-ISIS, undated), pp. 13–15.

[42] *IHT*, 22 July 1991.

[43] *China News* (Taipei), 21 November 1992.

[44] *The Straits Times*, 23 July 1991.

[45] *New Straits Times*, 24 July 1991.

[46] *Ibid.*, 3 December 1991.

[47] *The Environment and Human Rights in International Relations*.

[48] *The Straits Times*, 17 September 1991.

[49] 'Malaysia's Row With Singapore', *The Economist Foreign Report*, 24 September 1991, p. 6.

[50] *The Straits Times*, 21 June 1991, and 8 June 1991.

[51] *Ibid.*, 1 January 1992; *IHT*, 10 July 1991; *The Straits Times*, 22 July 1991.

[52] Paridan Abdul Samad and Darusalam Abu Bakar, 'Malaysia–Philippine Relations: The Issue of Sabah', *Asian Survey*, vol. 32, no. 6, June 1992, pp. 554–67.

[53] *The Straits Times*, editorial, 13 November 1987; *The Sunday Times* (Singapore), 16 April 1989.

[54] *The Straits Times*, 18 May 1989.

[55] Commodore Ahmad Ramli Nor, 'ASEAN Maritime Cooperation', paper presented at the Defence Asia '89 conference, 'Towards Greater ASEAN

Military and Security Cooperation: Issues and Prospects', Singapore, 22–25 March 1989, pp. 2–6.
[56] Lee Yong Leng, 'The Malaysian–Philippine Maritime Dispute', *Contemporary Southeast Asia*, vol. 11, no. 1, June 1989, pp. 61–74.
[57] *The Straits Times*, 14 September 1988.
[58] *Ibid.*, 17 August 1990.
[59] Simon, 'The Regionalization of Defence in Southeast Asia', p. 113.
[60] This point has been forcefully raised by Michael Leifer, 'Debating Asian Security: Michael Leifer Responds to Geoffrey Wiseman', *Pacific Review*, vol. 5, no. 2, 1992, p. 169.
[61] Noordin Sopiee, 'ASEAN and Regional Security', in Ayoob (ed.), *Regional Security in the Third World*, p. 228.
[62] Shamsudin Dubi, 'Security Trends in Southeast Asia: Implications for Regional Cooperation', paper presented to the international conference on 'Regional Cooperation in the Pacific Era', Yonsei University, Seoul, South Korea, 24–25 November 1987, p. 7.
[63] Chi-Kin Lo, *China's Policy Towards Territorial Disputes: The Case of the South China Sea Islands* (London: Routledge, 1989), p. 138.
[64] Hans Indorf, *The Spratlys: A Test Case for the Philippine Bases* (Manila: Centre for Research and Communication, May 1988), p. 14.
[65] Lee Lai To, 'The South China Sea Conflicts in the Post-Cold War Era', in *Proceedings of the Workshop on Managing Potential Conflicts in the South China Sea*, Bandung, 15–18 July 1991, pp. 172–73.
[66] Paul MacDonald, 'Scrambling for Oil in Asia', *The World Today*, vol. 48, no. 10, October 1992, p. 175.
[67] See Mark J. Valencia, 'Solving the Spratlys', *Pacific Research*, vol. 3, no. 2, May 1990, pp. 10–11.
[68] Hurng-yu Chen, 'The Prospect for Joint Development in the South China Sea', *Issues and Studies*, vol. 27, no. 12, December 1991, pp. 112–25.
[69] *Asia–Pacific Defence Reporter*, vol. 18, no. 2, August 1991, p. 18.
[70] Cited in Indorf, *The Spratlys*, p. 17.
[71] Ali Alatas, 'Managing the Potentials of the South China Sea', *Indonesian Quarterly*, vol. 18, no. 2, April 1990, p. 114.
[72] Address by Ali Alatas at the opening of the Second Workshop on 'Managing Potential Conflicts in the South China Sea', Bandung, 15 July 1991, p. 65.
[73] J. Soedjati Djiwandono, Preface to Special Issue on 'South China Sea Views from ASEAN', *Indonesian Quarterly*, vol. 18, no. 2, April 1990, p. 102.
[74] Donald K. Emmerson, 'Scenarios and Regimes', in Donald K. Emmerson and Sheldon W. Simon, *Regional Issues in Southeast Asian Security: Scenarios and Regimes*, study presented at the Third Annual Workshop on Asian Politics, Defense Intelligence College/National Bureau of Asian Research, California, 18–19 March 1993, p. 40.
[75] James A. Morse, 'ASEAN Focuses Concern on Spratly Islands Issue', *Wireless File* (East Asia and Pacific), United States Information Service (USIS), 23 July 1992, pp. 2–3.
[76] *New Straits Times*, 29 November 1985; *The Star*, 29 November 1985.
[77] FBIS-EAS-92-124, 26 June 1992, p. 34. Occasional piracy attacks have also been reported off the Natuna islands in the South China Sea, and in the Malawali channel in the Malaysian state of Sabah. The following is a break-down of reported piracy incidents in the region for 1991: Phillip Channel/Singapore Straits (65); Karimata Strait (6); South China Sea (19); Strait of Malacca (3); the Philippines coast (6); the Vietnamese coast (2); and the Bangladesh coast (1). See Commodore Sutedjo, Director of Naval Operations and Training, Indonesian Navy, 'Workable Operational Structures to Combat Piracy Activities in the Region (Southeast Asia)', paper presented to

the conference on 'Piracy in South-East Asia', organised by the Asian Investment Conferences (Pte) Ltd, Kuala Lumpur, 28–29 July 1992, p. 6.
[78] *The Straits Times*, 23 August 1992.
[79] *Ibid.*, 16 April 1993.
[80] 'Checking A Menace', *ibid.*, 31 July 1992.
[81] *Special Report: Piracy* (London: International Maritime Bureau, June 1992), pp. 10–11.
[82] FBIS-EAS-92-100, 22 May 1992, pp. 17–18.
[83] *The Straits Times*, 31 July 1992.
[84] Commodore Sutedjo, 'Workable Operational Structures', pp. 7–8.
[85] *The Straits Times*, 13 October 1992.
[86] FBIS-EAS-92-017, 27 January 1992, p. 6.
[87] Desmond Ball, 'Blueprint for Collective Security', *Asia–Pacific Defence Reporter*, vol. 18, no. 1, July 1991, p. 24.
[88] *Regional Piracy Centre* (London: International Maritime Bureau, 1992).
[89] *The Straits Times*, 2 October 1992.
[90] Commodore Sutedjo, 'Workable Operational Structures', p. 8.
[91] Edison Simandjutak, Head of Marine Patrol Section, Indonesia, 'Prevention and Control', paper presented to the conference on 'Piracy in South-East Asia'.

Chapter III

[1] For an overview of the domestic and external factors behind Vietnamese reform, see Robert G. Sutter, *Vietnam in Transition: Implications for US Policy* (Washington, DC: The Library of Congress, Congressional Research Service, 1989).
[2] Carlyle A. Thayer, 'The Challenges Facing Vietnamese Communism', *Southeast Asian Affairs 1992* (Singapore: Institute of Southeast Asian Studies, 1992), p. 352.
[3] *IHT*, 16 June 1987.
[4] For a discussion of Chatichai's initiative, see Leszek Buszynski, 'New Aspirations and Old Constraints in Thailand's Foreign Policy', *Asian Survey*, vol. 29, no. 11, November 1989, pp. 1057–72; Katharaya Um, 'Thailand and the Dynamics of Economics and Security Complex in Southeast Asia', *Contemporary Southeast Asia*, vol. 13, no. 3, December 1991, pp. 245–70.
[5] Dorothea Arndt, 'Foreign Assistance and Economic Policies in Laos', *Contemporary Southeast Asia*, vol. 14, no. 2, September 1992, p. 200.
[6] Donald Weatherbee, 'ASEAN the Big Loser in Thai Race for Profit in Indochina', *The Straits Times*, 5 May 1989.
[7] S. Rajaratnam, 'Riding the Vietnamese Tiger', *Contemporary Southeast Asia*, vol. 10, no. 4, March 1989, pp. 343–61.
[8] Cited in *The Straits Times*, 2 June 1989.
[9] *IHT*, 26 January 1989, and 30 January 1989; *The Straits Times*, 14 March 1989.
[10] Paisal Srichratchanya, 'Wait and See', *Far Eastern Economic Review*, 11 May 1989, p. 21.
[11] See Muthiah Alagappa, 'Bringing Indochina into Asean', *ibid.*, 29 June 1989, pp. 21–22.
[12] *Bangkok Post*, 16 December 1988.
[13] *The Straits Times*, 14 January 1989.
[14] *Ibid.*, 17 January 1991.
[15] *Ibid.*, 13 December 1990.
[16] *Ibid.*, 23 November 1990.
[17] *IHT*, 21 March 1989. The Vietnamese desire to join ASEAN was clearly conveyed to the visiting Foreign Secretary of the Philippines, Raul Manglapus, by Party Chairman Nguyen Van Linh and Foreign Minister Nguyen Co Thach in November 1988. See *The Straits Times*, 18 April 1989.
[18] Cited in Frank Frost, 'Vietnam and Asean: From Enmity to Cooperation', *Trends*, 29 December 1991, p. 26.
[19] *Ibid.*
[20] For a comprehensive discussion of the factors behind economic reform in Laos, see William Worner, 'Economic

Reform and Structural Change In Laos', in *Southeast Asian Affairs 1989* (Singapore: Institute of Southeast Asian Studies, 1989), pp. 187–208.

[21] Martin Stuart-Fox, 'Laos 1991: On the Offensive', in *Southeast Asian Affairs 1992*, p. 177.

[22] The Final Act of the Paris Peace Conference, signed on 23 October 1991, consists of three documents: 'An Agreement on a Comprehensive Political Settlement of the Cambodia Conflict'; 'An Agreement Concerning the Sovereignty, Independence, Territorial Integrity and Inviolability, Neutrality and National Unity of Cambodia'; and a 'Declaration on the Rehabilitation and Reconstruction of Cambodia'. The first document contained annexes on 'the mandate for UNTAC, military matters, elections, repatriation of Cambodian refugees and displaced persons, and the principles for a new Cambodian constitution'.

[23] See Michael Leifer, 'Power-sharing and Peacemaking in Cambodia', *SAIS Review*, vol. 12, no. 1, Winter–Spring 1992, pp. 139–53.

[24] Text of statement by Datuk Abdullah Ahmad Badawi at the Paris Peace Conference on Cambodia, 23 October 1991, p. 2.

[25] Goh Chok Tong, 'Towards a Positive Relationship With Vietnam', *Speeches* (Singapore Ministry of Information and the Arts), vol. 15, no. 5, September–October 1991, p. 9.

[26] Douglas Pike, 'Vietnam in 1991: The Turning Point', *Asian Survey*, vol. 32, no. 2, January 1992, p. 81.

[27] *The Straits Times*, 17 February 1992.

[28] *Ibid.*

[29] FBIS-EAS-92-025, 6 February 1992, pp. 43–44.

[30] Surin Maisrikrod, 'Thailand and the Indochinese Conundrum', *Trends*, 23 February 1992, p. 25.

[31] International Monetary Fund, *Direction of Trade Statistics Yearbook*, as reported in Mya Than, 'ASEAN, Indochina and Myanmar: Towards Economic Cooperation', *ASEAN Economic Bulletin*, vol. 8, no. 2, November 1991, p. 183.

[32] *The Straits Times*, 22 April 1992.

[33] *Ibid.*, 3 July 1992.

[34] 'Creating the Marketplace', *Bangkok Post Year End Review*, 1991.

[35] *New Straits Times*, 20 April 1992.

[36] *Regional Outlook 1991* (Singapore: Institute of Southeast Asian Studies, 1991), p. 58.

[37] Indeed, Malaysian investment in Vietnam was put at $67.5m on the eve of Prime Minister Mahathir's visit in April 1991. See *New Straits Times*, 20 April 1992.

[38] *The Straits Times*, 6 July 1992.

[39] *Ibid.*, 3 July 1992.

[40] *Vietnam, Laos and Cambodia in Transition: Reconstruction and Economic Development*, vol. 1, overview and summary of a workshop organised by the Sasakawa Peace Foundation, Tokyo, 8–11 November 1991, p. 38.

[41] Dorothy Teoh, '2006: An ASEAN Odyssey to Free Trade', *ASEAN-ISIS Monitor*, no. 2, January 1992, p. 10.

[42] During the Singapore summit, Thailand's interim Prime Minister Anand Panyarachun argued that 'there is no need to rush them [the Indochinese states] into becoming members' until 'the level of their economic system becomes more compatible with ours'. See *The Straits Times*, 17 February 1992.

[43] Narongchai Akrasanee in *ibid.*

[44] *The Straits Times*, 13 December 1990.

[45] Cited in Thu My, 'Renovation in Vietnam and Its Effects on Peace, Friendship and Cooperation in Southeast Asia', in Nguen Duy Quy (ed.), *Unity in Diversity: Cooperation Between Vietnam and Other Southeast Asian Countries* (Hanoi: Social Science Publishing House, 1992), pp. 141–42.

[46] Martin Gainsborough, 'Vietnam II: A Turbulent Normalisation with China', *The World Today*, vol. 48, no. 11, November 1992, p. 207.

[47] *The Straits Times*, 21 July 1992.

[48] Frost, 'Vietnam and ASEAN', p. 26.
[49] One analyst has envisaged Vietnamese membership of ASEAN by the end of 1994. See Gainsborough, 'Vietnam II', p. 207.
[50] Translated and reproduced as 'Main Security Concerns in Southeast Asia', *The Straits Times*, 25 March 1992.
[51] Michael Vatikiotis, 'Join the Club', *Far Eastern Economic Review*, 20 June 1991, p. 26.
[52] Amitav Acharya, 'Arms Proliferation Issues in ASEAN: Towards a Conventional Defence Posture?' *Contemporary Southeast Asia*, vol. 10, no. 3, December 1988, p. 246.
[53] *The Straits Times*, 18 February 1992.
[54] This was acknowledged by Thai Prime Minister Panyarachun: 'ASEAN members are free to determine their own policies *vis-à-vis* Indochina. We need more consultations with each other, but it does not mean we need to have a common policy'.
[55] Mike Yeong, 'ASEAN's New Challenge in Indochina', *Trends*, 23 February 1992, p. 25.
[56] See Surin Maisrikrod, 'Thailand and the Indochina Conundrum', p. 25. A Thai diplomat recently warned that 'good relations among ASEAN countries can be adversely affected if initiatives on Indochina are undertaken by any ASEAN member without prior consultation with other ASEAN members'. See Asda Jayanama, 'One Southeast Asia: The Issues at Stake', *Vietnam Commentary*, no. 24, November–December 1991, p. 38.
[57] Keynote address by Datuk Abdullah Ahmad Badawi at the 4th Southeast Asia Forum, Kuala Lumpur, 16 January 1992, p. 7.
[58] See Donald Weatherbee, 'Thailand in 1989: Democracy Ascendant in the Golden Peninsula', in *Southeast Asian Affairs 1990* (Singapore: Institute of Southeast Asian Studies, 1990), pp. 349–50.

Chapter IV

[1] Adam Malik, 'Regional Cooperation in International Politics', in *Regionalism in Southeast Asia* (Jakarta: CSIS, 1975), p. 160.
[2] *New Straits Times*, 11 January 1978.
[3] Noordin Sopiee, 'The Neutralisation of Southeast Asia', in Hedley Bull (ed.), *Asia and the Western Pacific: Towards a New International Order* (Melbourne and Sydney: Thomas Nelson, 1975), p. 144.
[4] Mohammed Ghazalie bin Shafie, 'The Neutralisation of Southeast Asia', *Pacific Community*, vol. 3, no. 1, October 1971, p. 115.
[5] Muthiah Alagappa, *Towards a Nuclear-Weapons-Free Zone in Southeast Asia*, ISIS Research Note (Kuala Lumpur: Institute of Strategic and International Studies, 1987).
[6] *New Straits Times*, 3 February 1988.
[7] Muthiah Alagappa, 'Regional Arrangements and International Security in Southeast Asia', *Contemporary Southeast Asia*, vol. 12, no. 4, March 1991, pp. 269–305.
[8] *The Straits Times* (editorial), 1 February 1992.
[9] Keynote address by Ali Alatas to the United Nations Regional Disarmament Workshop for Asia and Pacific, in *Disarmament* (New York: United Nations Department for Disarmament Affairs, 1991), p. 14. In addition, an Indonesian scholar, Jusuf Wanandi, has pointed to the continuing validity of ZOPFAN in the following respects: '(a) as a foundation for the creation of a peaceful and stable regional order involving the ten Southeast Asian countries, particularly in a wider Asia–Pacific regional environment that had become truly multipolar; (b) as a framework . . . for developing a relationship between ASEAN and the Indochinese countries . . . ; (c) as a political leverage for ASEAN (and the other Southeast Asian countries) in its active participation in the wider Pacific regional cooperation scheme'. See Jusuf

Wanandi, 'Towards a New Regional Order for ASEAN', paper presented to the symposium on 'The Changing Role of the United Nations in Conflict Resolution and Peace-keeping', pp. 3–4.
[10] Bilveer Singh, *ZOPFAN and the New Security Order in Asia–Pacific* (Petaling Jaya: Pelanduk Publications, 1991), p. 98.
[11] *The Straits Times*, 31 December 1990.
[12] 'Live and Let Live', p. 13.
[13] Michael Vatikiotis, 'Permanent Presence', *Far Eastern Economic Review*, 16 January 1992, p. 22.
[14] *The Straits Times*, 17 April 1992.
[15] *Ibid.*, 10 April 1992 and 13 February 1992.
[16] *Ibid.*, 10 April 1992.
[17] *Ibid.*, 14 April 1992.
[18] *The Straits Times*, 25 July 1991.
[19] Michael Richardson, 'Indonesia–US Get Together', *Asia–Pacific Defence Reporter*, vol. 18, nos 10/11, April–May 1992, p. 31.
[20] *The Straits Times*, 10 April 1992.
[21] Chin Kin Wah, 'The Five-Power Defence Arrangements: Twenty Years After', *The Pacific Review*, vol. 4, no. 3, 1991, pp. 193–203.
[22] Ball, 'Blueprint for Collective Security', pp. 24–26.
[23] *The Straits Times* (weekly overseas edition), 9 December 1989. For an overview of the role of the FPDA in ASEAN security, see, K.U. Menon, 'A Six-Power Defence Arrangement in Southeast Asia', *Contemporary Southeast Asia*, vol. 10, no. 3, December 1988, pp. 306–27.
[24] *The Straits Times*, 14 April 1992.
[25] *IHT*, 31 October–1 November 1992. See also Mochtar Kusumaatmadja, 'Some Thoughts on ASEAN Security Cooperation: An Indonesian Perspective', *Contemporary Southeast Asia*, vol. 12, no. 3, December 1990, pp. 161–71.
[26] *The Straits Times*, 21 February 1991.
[27] Michael Vatikiotis, 'Time for Decisions', *Far Eastern Economic Review*, 16 January 1992, pp. 23–24.
[28] On the concept of common security, see Olof Palme, *Common Security: A Blueprint for Survival* (New York: Simon and Schuster, 1982); The Palme Commission on Disarmament and Security Issues, *A World at Peace: Common Security in the Twenty-first Century* (Stockholm: The Palme Commission, 1989); SIPRI, *Policies for Common Security* (London: Taylor and Francis, 1985). Common security emphasises the role of confidence- and security-building measures (CSBMs) among adversaries. The classic model for regional common security is the Conference on Security and Cooperation in Europe (CSCE). See Volker Rittberger, Manfred Efinger and Martin Mendler, 'Toward an East–West Security Regime: The Case of Confidence- and Security-Building Measures', *Journal of Peace Research*, vol. 27, no. 1, January 1990, pp. 55–74. For a good evaluation of the prospects for common security in the Asia–Pacific context, see Geoffrey Wiseman, 'Common Security in the Asia–Pacific Region', *Pacific Review*, vol. 5, no. 1, 1992, pp. 42–59.
[29] The problems of applying European-style CSBMs to the Asia–Pacific region are discussed in Trevor Findlay, 'Confidence-building Measures for the Asia–Pacific: The Relevance of the European Experience', in M. Alagappa (ed.), *Building Confidence-Resolving Conflicts* (Kuala Lumpur: Institute for International and Strategic Studies, 1989), pp. 55–74; For a survey of regional attitudes towards CSBMs at this time, see Findlay, *Asia–Pacific CSBMs: A Prospectus* (Canberra: Australian National University, Peace Research Centre, 1990).
[30] 'Asian Security in the 1990s: Integration in Economics: Diversity in Defense', speech by Richard Solomon, Assistant Secretary of State for East Asian and Pacific Affairs, at the

University of San Diego, 30 October 1990, excerpts published in the *US Department of State Dispatch*, 5 November 1990. Solomon argued that 'East Asia is a region so vastly different from Europe in terms of its history, cultural diversity, levels of economic development and geopolitical architecture that imposing the logic of European security is simply inappropriate. The Cold War did not weld the region into two opposing blocs and there is no single threat commonly perceived across the region. Instead, there is a multiplicity of security concerns that vary from one subregion to another'.

[31] *The Straits Times*, 7 August 1991.

[32] Excerpts from Lee Kuan Yew's interview in *The Australian*, published in *The Straits Times*, 16 September 1988. See also Michael Vatikiotis, 'Yankee Please Stay', *Far Eastern Economic Review*, 13 December 1990, p. 32. It is also noteworthy that ASEAN states opposed a security role for the Asia–Pacific Economic Cooperation (APEC) framework. APEC was proposed by the then Australian Prime Minister Bob Hawke in January 1989 as a formal intergovernmental vehicle for cooperation allowing the region as a whole to coordinate an approach to the General Agreement on Tariffs and Trade (GATT) and increase the liberalisation of trade in the area. ASEAN's initial attitude towards APEC was one of extreme caution, bordering on rejection. Like the idea of a CSCA, APEC was viewed as a competitor to ASEAN in its role as a vehicle for regional cooperation in the Asia–Pacific region. Indonesian Foreign Minister Ali Alatas wanted APEC meetings to focus on the annual ASEAN PMC sessions. The idea would not be endorsed until four conditions were met: APEC should not deal with political and security issues; it should not lead to the formation of a trade bloc; its institutional arrangements should not reduce the importance and role of existing Asia–Pacific institutions for cooperation; and ASEAN's machinery should be the centre of the APEC process.

[33] *The Straits Times*, 22 July 1991.

[34] *Ibid.*, 10 July 1991.

[35] Excerpts from Lee Kuan Yew's interview in *The Australian*, published in *The Straits Times*, 16 September 1988.

[36] Sukhumbhand Paribatra, 'Meeting the Challenge of the Post-Cold War World: Some Reflections on the Making of a New Southeast Asia', paper presented to the Fourth Southeast Asian Forum, organised by the Institute of Strategic and International Studies, Kuala Lumpur, Malaysia, 15–18 January 1992, pp. 24–25.

[37] Cited in Michael Vatikiotis, 'The New Player', *Far Eastern Economic Review*, 1 August 1991, p. 11.

[38] *The Sunday Times* (Singapore), 21 July 1991; *IHT*, 22 and 23 July 1991.

[39] See 'A Time for Initiative', *ASEAN-ISIS Monitor*, no. 1, July 1991, pp. 2–3. See also Lau Teik Soon, *Towards a Regional Security Conference: Role of the Non-Government Organizations*, Working Papers no. 1 (Singapore: Department of Political Science, National University of Singapore, 1991).

[40] Jane A. Morse, 'US Pleased with ASEAN's Attention to Regional Security', *Wireless File* (East Asia and Pacific), USIS, Singapore, 24 July 1992, p. 8.

[41] *Provisional Agenda of ASEAN Post-Ministerial Conferences (PMC)*, Manila, 27–29 July 1992.

[42] *Asian Wall Street Journal*, 23 July 1992.

[43] Michael Vatikiotis, 'Action at Last', *Far Eastern Economic Review*, 6 February 1992, p. 11.

[44] James A. Baker, 'America in Asia: Emerging Architecture for a Pacific Community', *Foreign Affairs*, vol. 70, no. 5, Winter 1991–92, p. 5.

[45] 'Places, Not Bases: Pacific Com-

mander Outlines New US Defence Role', *Far Eastern Economic Review*, 22 April 1993, p. 22.

[46] Brian L. Job and Frank Langdon, *The Evolving Security Order of the Asia–Pacific: A Canadian Perspective*, North Pacific Cooperative Security Dialogue Working Paper no. 15 (Toronto: York University, Centre for International and Strategic Studies, 1992), p. 27.

[47] See Gerald Segal, 'North-East Asia: Common Security or à la carte?', *International Affairs*, vol. 67, no. 4, October 1991, pp. 755–67.

[48] 'Low Key Diplomacy', *Far Eastern Economic Review*, 14 January 1993, p. 12.

[49] See Wiseman, 'Common Security in the Asia–Pacific Region'.

[50] In this context, the Canadian Initiative for a North Pacific Cooperative Security Dialogue deserves notice. For an appraisal of the Canadian initiative, see Stewart Henderson, *Canada and Asia Pacific Security: The North Pacific Cooperative Security Dialogue*, Policy Planning Staff paper no. 92/3 (Ottawa: External Affairs and International Trade Canada, 1992).

[51] *Asian Wall Street Journal*, 27 July 1992.

[52] See Tim Huxley, 'South-East Asia's Arms Race: Some Notes on Recent Developments', *Arms Control*, vol. 11, no. 1, May 1990, pp. 69–76; Michael Vatikiotis, 'Measure for Measure: Malaysia, Singapore, Poised to Acquire New Arms', *Far Eastern Economic Review*, 30 April 1992, p. 18; John Dikkenberg, 'The Arms Race', *Asiaweek*, 19–21 June 1992, pp. 11–19.

[53] Some countries in the region do not include internal security expenditure in their defence budget, while others do. Several countries use special funds to import weapons which are not reported in official allocations for defence.

[54] For example, data compiled by a Japanese scholar based on current dollars and exchange rates indicates a dramatic growth in regional defence expenditure during the period 1989–90. In the case of Thailand, the increase in its defence budget in 1992 was 13.5% over the level in 1991, 30.8% over that in 1990 and 55% over 1989. Singapore's 1992 defence budget represents an 11.6% increase over actual defence expenditure in 1991, 20.3% over 1990 and 40.9% over 1989. In the case of Malaysia, defence expenditure in 1992 increased by 21.8% over 1991, while for Indonesia, the 1992 defence budget was 14.1% over that for the previous year. The defence budget of the Philippines for 1992 was about 42.9% higher than that for 1989. See Shigekatsu Kondo, 'The Evolving Security Environment: Political', paper presented to the conference on 'Arms Control and Confidence-Building in the Asia-Pacific Region', organised by the Canadian Institute for International Peace and Security, Ottawa, 22–23 May 1992, pp. 4–5. See also Andrew Mack, 'Asia's New Military Build-up', *Pacific Research*, February 1991, p. 12.

[55] *Far Eastern Economic Review*, 24–31 December 1992, p. 20.

[56] *The Straits Times*, 11 July 1991.

[57] *Ibid.*, 27 March 1992.

[58] FBIS-EAS-92-020, 30 January 1992, p. 53.

[59] In February 1992, the interim Thai Prime Minister, Anand Panyarachun, stated that in the absence of a security threat in the region, Thailand 'should look at its defence spending programme'. See FBIS-EAS-92-022, 3 February 1992, p. 69.

[60] These details can be found in Leszek Buszynski, 'ASEAN Security Dilemmas', *Survival*, vol. 34, no. 4, Winter 1992–93, pp. 90–107; Sheldon Simon, *The Regionalization of Defence in Southeast Asia* (Seattle, WA: The National Bureau of Asian Research, 1992). See also, 'Southeast Asian Navies Modernise', *Pacific Research*, vol. 4, no. 2, May 1991, p. 10; Robert Karniol, 'Asian Build-up: Regional Powers Strengthen Their Hand',

International Defense Review, vol. 24, no. 6, June 1991, pp. 611–12; 'Brunei Decides on UK Hawk Buy', *Jane's Defence Weekly*, 12 October 1991, p. 657; Robert Karniol, 'Thailand's Armed Forces: From Counter-insurgency to Conventional Warfare', *International Defense Review*, vol. 25, no. 2, February 1992, pp. 97–106; Robert Karniol, 'Philippines Plans Trainer Buy', *Jane's Defence Weekly*, 1 February 1992, p. 146; 'ASEAN Plus Special Report: Options for Defence', *ibid.*, 22 February 1992, pp. 293–310; 'AMX Locks Talons with Hawk', *International Defense Review*, vol. 25, no. 4, April 1992, p. 371; 'Fulcrum Awaits F-5E/F Decision', *Jane's Defence Weekly*, 9 May 1992, p. 798; David Foxwell, 'Far East Navies', *International Defense Review*, vol. 25, no. 2, February 1992, pp. 123–31; Joris Janssen Lok, 'Malaysia to Buy UK-Built Frigates', *Jane's Defence Weekly*, 11 April 1992, p. 607; Joris Janssen Lok, 'Blue Water Navies: Flagship Fleets of Asia-Pacific', *ibid.*, pp. 622–24.

[61] Andrew Mack and Desmond Ball, 'The Military Build-up in the Asia-Pacific', *Pacific Review*, vol. 5, no. 3, 1992, p. 199.

[62] In the words of the former chief of Malaysia's defence forces: 'there is no arms race here and I am sure one will not occur', *The Straits Times*, 25 July 1992.

[63] Opening address by Dr Yeo Ning Hong, Singapore's Minister for Defence, at the First Asia–Pacific Defence Conference, Singapore, 26 February 92, pp. 2–3.

[64] Cited in Michael Vatikiotis, 'Assessing the Threat', *Far Eastern Economic Review*, 20 June 1991, p. 29.

[65] See Ron Huisken, *Limitation of Armaments in Southeast Asia: A Proposal* (Canberra: Strategic and Defence Studies Centre, Australian National University, 1977); Susanne M. Feske, *ASEAN and Prospects for Regional Arms Control in Southeast Asia* (Berlin: Quorom Verlag, 1986); Lew Eng Fee, 'Arms Control in Southeast Asia: A Review of the Debate', *Contemporary Southeast Asia*, vol. 10, no. 3, December 1988; Charles Van Der Donckt, *The Changing Naval Environment in Southeast Asia*, Extramural paper no. 56 (Ottawa: Department of National Defence, Operational Research and Analysis Establishment, 1991), pp. 115–17.

[66] Andrew Mack, 'Naval Arms Control and Confidence-Building for Northeast Asian Waters', paper presented at the conference on 'Arms Control and Confidence-Building in the Asia–Pacific Region', p. 4.

[67] *The Straits Times*, 25 August 1992.

[68] Lt-General Winston Choo, Commander of Singapore's Armed Forces, interviewed in the *Asian Defence Journal*, no. 3, March 1989, p. 46.

[69] *The Straits Times*, 5 May 1989; *The Sunday Times* (Singapore), 14 May 1989.

[70] Leszek Buszynski, 'Southeast Asia in the Post-Cold War Era: Regionalism and Security', *Asian Survey*, vol. 32, no. 9, September 1992, p. 840.

[71] Subsequent to the proposal for a 'defence community' by the then Foreign Minister of Malaysia, the country's Chief of Defence Forces, General Hashim Mohammed Ali, outlined six factors which must be taken into account in any move by the ASEAN countries towards cooperation on regional defence: the members must benefit militarily, politically, economically and socially from the cooperation; the long-term objective of ZOPFAN must be adhered to which means phasing out extraregional powers; the achievement of regional peace should not be at the expense of creating or inciting unnecessary fear among the non-participants, i.e., extra-ASEAN powers; there must be continued preservation of an individual member's right to self-determination and sover-

eignty; the question of affordability, i.e., expenditure on defence, must not jeopardise the need for economic development; the form of cooperation must be in concert with the current and foreseeable future international environment. These conditions are a useful reminder of the obstacles facing any ASEAN 'defence community'. For the full text of the General's remarks, see *ISIS Focus* (newsletter of the Institute of Strategic and International Studies, Malaysia), no. 58, January 1990.

[72] 'Is ASEAN Turning Into a Military Pact?', *Asian Defence Journal*, no. 5, May 1989, p. 113.

[73] Text of address by General Hashim Mohammed Ali at a Seminar organised by the Integrated Air Defence System in Singapore, 29 November 1989, 'Regional Defence From the Military Perspective', *ISIS Focus*, no. 58, January 1990, p. 42.

[74] FBIS-EAS-92-017, 27 January 1992, p. 1.

[75] 'Promoting Bilateral Cooperation Between Singapore and Indonesia', *Pioneer*, no. 138, April 1989, pp. 2–3; *The Straits Times*, 24 March 1989.

[76] FBIS-EAS-92-033, 19 February 1992, p. 54.

[77] Mochtar Kusumaatmatdja, 'Some Thoughts on ASEAN Security Cooperation: An Indonesian Perspective', *Contemporary Southeast Asia*, vol. 12, no. 3, December 1990, pp. 161–71.

[78] *The Straits Times* (weekly overseas edition), 17 February 1990.

[79] 'Blood and Money', *Far Eastern Economic Review*, 1 March 1990, p. 9.

[80] '10 Years of Training in Brunei', *Pioneer*, no. 124, February 1988.

[81] *The Straits Times*, 22 August 1986.

[82] *Bangkok Post*, 17 July 1983; *New Straits Times*, 18 July 1983.

[83] *The Straits Times*, 20 February 1992; FBIS-EAS-92-033, 19 February 1992, p. 45.

[84] *The Business Times* (Kuala Lumpur), 13 May 1989.

[85] *The Straits Times*, 21 April 1989.

[86] *Bangkok Post*, 27 January 1988.

[87] *The Straits Times*, 20 February 1992.

[88] J.N. Mak, *Directions for Greater Defence Cooperation* (Kuala Lumpur: Institute of Strategic and International Studies, 1986), p. 22.

[89] *The Straits Times*, 5 May 1988.

[90] Mak, *Directions for Greater Defence Cooperation*, p. 22.

[91] Robert Karniol, 'ASEAN's Need for Greater Defence Cooperation', *Jane's Defence Weekly*, 10 November 1988.

[92] *The Straits Times*, 17 July 1987. See also Bilveer Singh, 'ASEAN's Arms Industries: Potential and Limits', *Comparative Strategy*, vol. 8, no. 2, 1989, pp. 249–64.

[93] Rodolfo C. Garcia, 'Military Cooperation in ASEAN', *The Pointer*, vol. 14, no. 2, April–June 1988, pp. 9–10.

[94] John McBeth, 'On the Defensive', *Far Eastern Economic Review*, 20 June 1991, p. 26.

[95] FBIS-EAS-92-019, 29 January 1992, p. 5.